When the first baby laughed for the first time,

His laugh broke into a million pieces,

And they all went skipping about.

That was the beginning of fairies.

J.M. Barrie, Little White Bird., Ch. 16

EMBROIDERED

Christening Gowns

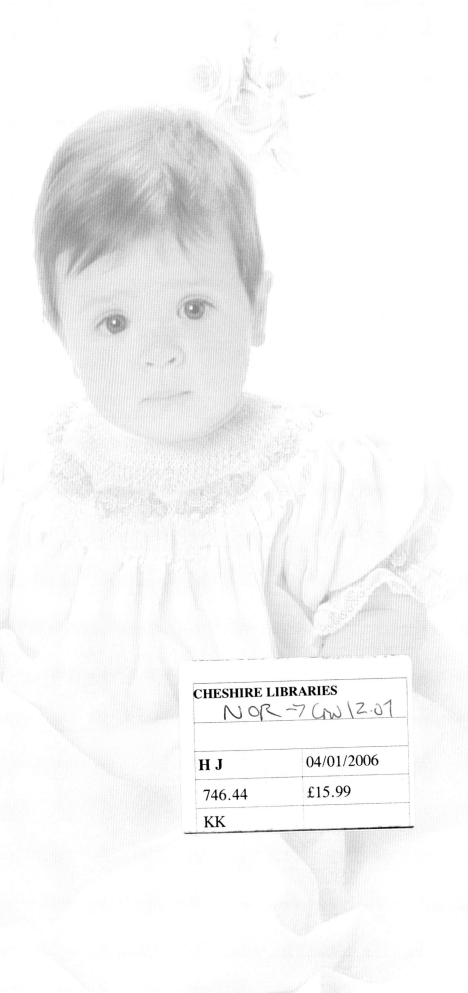

CONTENTS

4

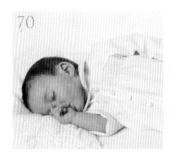

INSPIRATIONS BOOKS

EDITOR Sue Gardner
GRAPHIC DESIGN Lynton Grandison
ILLUSTRATIONS Kathy Barac
PHOTOGRAPHY Andrew Dunbar
REPROGRAPHICS PrintX Digital
PUBLISHER Margie Bauer

EMBROIDERED CHRISTENING GOWNS
ISBN 0-9750920-1-4
COPYRIGHT © 2005
COUNTRY BUMPKIN PUBLICATIONS
ADELAIDE, AUSTRALIA

INTRODUCTION

Making the decision to have a child is momentous.

It is to decide forever to have your heart go on walking around outside your body.

ELIZABETH STONE

Some of the most precious moments of our lives revolve around our children and there is no moment more special than the birth of a babe.

A christening is a celebration of that precious life, a rich and joyous event that affirms our belief in the future and a love that is indescribable to anyone but a parent.

The breathtaking garments within this book are indeed gifts of love. The act of selflessly creating a thing of beauty for a cherished child truly embraces the meaning of giving.

Thank you to the wonderful women who have contributed their talents and time to create these garments and share them with you. I hope their work and this book bring you much pleasure in reading, in stitching, in giving and in creating beautiful memories of a life just beginning.

Welcome to the special little person entering your world.

Sue Gardner EDITOR

*As delicate as rose petals, this beautiful gown of pure white tulle is
adorned with lace and dainty ribbon embroidery. A lace trimmed
petticoat is worn beneath the gown. The sweet tulle bonnet is finished
with ruffles of lace and ties with soft satin ribbons.*

Sizes 3, 6 & 12 months

GOWN, BONNET & PETTICOAT

REQUIREMENTS

Fabric & Lace

White cotton tulle
3.8m x 145cm wide (4yd 5 5/8" x 57")
for all sizes

White cotton batiste
1.6m x 112cm wide (1yd 27" x 44")
for all sizes

White organza
15cm x 10cm wide (6" x 4")
for all sizes

White cotton lace edging
14m x 30mm wide (15yd 11" x 1 1/8")

White cotton lace edging
2.6m x 8mm wide (2yd 30 3/8" x 5/16")

White cotton lace beading
11.5m x 12mm wide (12yd 21" x 1/2")

White cotton lace insertion
10.5m x 8mm wide (11yd 17" x 5/16")

Notions

25cm (10") white satin mini piping

Bridal white double sided satin ribbon
14m x 5mm wide (15yd 11" x 3/16")

2 white buttons 12mm (1/2") wide
for the gown

2 white buttons 10mm (3/8") wide
for the petticoat

White cotton heirloom machine
sewing thread

Fine water-soluble fabric marker

No. 10 crewel needle

No. 10 straw needle

Threads & Ribbons

YLI silk ribbon 7mm (5/16") wide
A = no. 3 bridal white 1.5m (1yd 23")

DMC stranded cotton
B = blanc

Anchor stranded silk
C = 926 cream

STITCHES & TECHNIQUES USED

BULLION KNOT

COLONIAL KNOT

FLY STITCH

GATHERED RIBBON FLOWER

ATTACHING FLAT LACE
TO FLAT LACE

ATTACHING LACE BEADING
TO NET

ATTACHING GATHERED LACE
TO FLAT LACE

the Gown

GOWN ONLY

REQUIREMENTS

Fabric & Lace

White cotton tulle
3.8m x 145cm wide (4yd 5 5/8" x 57")
for all sizes

White organza
15cm x 10cm wide (6" x 4")
for all sizes

White cotton lace edging
12m x 30mm wide (13yd 4" x 1 1/8")

White cotton lace beading
12m x 12mm wide (13yd 4" x 1/2")

White cotton lace insertion
8m x 8mm wide (8yd 27" x 5/16")

Notions

25cm (10") white satin mini piping

Bridal white double sided satin ribbon
13m x 5mm wide (14yd 14" x 3/16")

2 white buttons 12mm (1/2") wide

White cotton heirloom machine
sewing thread

Fine water-soluble fabric marker

No. 10 crewel needle

No. 10 straw needle

Threads & Ribbons

YLI silk ribbon 7mm (5/16") wide
A = no. 3 bridal white 90cm (35 1/2")

DMC stranded cotton
B = blanc

Anchor stranded silk
C = 926 cream

PATTERN & CUTTING OUT

See the liftout pattern sheet for the
pattern and cutting layout.

Cut out all other pieces following the
instructions on the liftout pattern sheet.

PREPARATION FOR EMBROIDERY

See the liftout pattern sheet for the
embroidery design.

Assemble the gown following the
instructions on pages 115 - 118.

Place clear plastic film over the
embroidery designs on the master
pattern, or alternatively, trace the
embroidery designs onto white paper
with a black pen.

Front yoke

Position the left hand side of the
front yoke over the corresponding
embroidery design, aligning the piping
and armhole seam with the placement
marks on the design. Using a water-
soluble fabric marker, mark the centre
of each flower with a dot. Repeat on
the right hand side.

Sleeves

Fold one sleeve in half to find the
centre. Mark the centre with a pin.
Position the sleeve over the
embroidery design ensuring the design
is centred between the lace insertion
and lace beading, and the central
flower aligns with the pin. Using the
fabric marker, mark the centre of each
flower with a dot. Repeat for the
second sleeve.

EMBROIDERY

Front yoke

Cut a piece of ribbon 11cm (4 5/8")
long. Leaving approximately 1cm (3/8")
at each end, mark the ribbon into five
17.5mm (7/8") sections (see diag 1).

Using fine heirloom sewing thread and
small stitches, work running stitch

along the ribbon following the diagram
below *(diag 1)*.

Diag I

Take the thread over the edge of the
ribbon each time before working the
parallel row of stitches. Pull up the
thread gently to form the petals.
Secure the threads on the back of the
flower and trim away any excess
ribbon if necessary. Fashion five more
ribbon flowers in the same manner.
Attach three ribbon flowers to each
side of the yoke at the marked
positions.

Stitch the bullion roses next, working
two bullion knots for the centre of
each one and surround with ten
bullion knots for the petals.

Work two bullion knots for each
rosebud, ensuring both knots use the
same holes in the fabric. Add two fly
stitches to each bud for the sepals.
Finally, stitch three colonial knots in
each design.

Sleeves

Fashion two gathered ribbon flowers
following the instructions for those on
the yoke. Attach a ribbon flower to
the centre mark and add 2 - 3 colonial
knots to the middle of the flower.

Work a white bullion rose and cream
bullion bud on each side of the ribbon
flower. Surround each bud with two
fly stitches for the sepals.

CONSTRUCTION

See pages 115 - 118.

The finished length of the gown from the centre back neckline to the hemline is 85cm (33 ½") for all sizes.

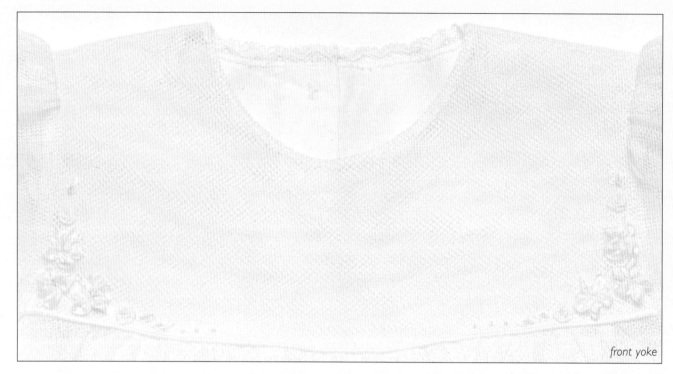

front yoke

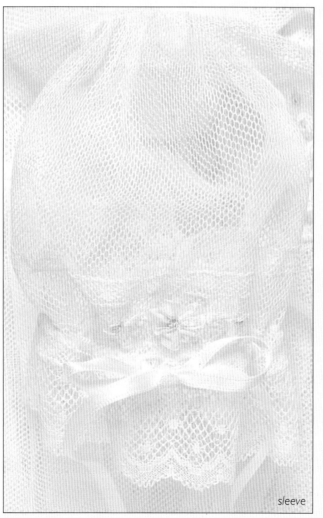

sleeve

skirt

Went to Bettws in the afternoon wrapped in two waistcoats, two coats, a muffler and a mackintosh, and was not at all too warm. Heard the Chapel bell pealing strongly for the second time since I have been here and when I got to the Chapel my beard moustaches and whiskers were so stiff with ice that I could hardly open my mouth and my beard was frozen on to my mackintosh.

There was a large christening party from Llwyn Gwilym. The clerk (Wilding) thrust a tallow candle between the bars of the stove grate lighted it and set it upon the table that once probably did duty for a Communion table. I had it put out again as the daylight was sufficient. The baby was baptized in ice which was broken and swimming about in the Font.

REV. FRANCIS KILVERT (1840 – 1879)

the *Petticoat*

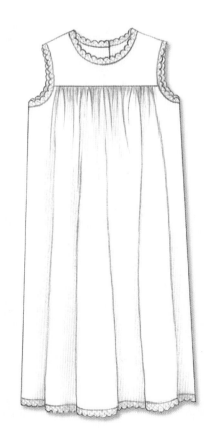

PETTICOAT ONLY

REQUIREMENTS

Fabric & Lace

White cotton batiste
1.6m x 112cm wide (1yd 27" x 44")
for all sizes

White cotton lace edging
1m x 8mm wide (1yd 3 ³/₈" x ⁵/₁₆")

White cotton lace edging
2m x 30mm wide (2yd 6 ³/₄" x 1 ¹/₈")

Notions

2 white buttons 10mm (¹/₂") wide

White cotton heirloom machine
sewing thread

Fine water-soluble fabric marker

PATTERN & CUTTING OUT

See the liftout pattern sheet for the pattern and cutting layout.

Cut out all pieces following the instructions on the liftout pattern sheet.

CONSTRUCTION

See pages 118 - 119.

EMBROIDERY KEY

All thread embroidery is worked with one strand.

Gathered ribbon flowers

Petals = A (gathered ribbon)

Centre (sleeves only) = C
(colonial knot)

Roses on yoke

Centre = C
(2 bullion knots, 7 wraps)

Petals = B (9 bullion knots,
10 - 12 wraps)

Roses on sleeves

Centre = B
(2 bullion knots, 7 wraps)

Inner petals = B
(4 bullion knots, 10 wraps)

Outer petals = B
(7 bullion knots, 12 wraps)

Rosebuds

Petals = C
(2 bullion knots, 6 wraps)

Sepals = B (fly stitch)

Spots = C (colonial knot)

Then every one of them, by order, gave their presents for the god-bairn gift. The jewels of precious stones the queen received in her own hand and then delivered then unto me (write Melville), to put them again in their cases, and lay them upon a table which was prepared in the midst of the chamber to set them upon.

The Queen of England's had a great show, being a fair cupboard of silver overgilt, cunningly wrought, and some cups of massy gold. The ambassadors of the states presented a golden box, wherein was written on parchment, in letters of gold, 'A gift of a yearly pension to the prince of five thousand... by year', with great cups of massy gold, two especially which were enough for me to lift and set them down upon the said table. I leave it to others to set down their weight and value.

SIR JAMES MELVILLE, ENVOY TO THE COURT OF ELIZABETH WRITES ABOUT THE PRESENTS RECEIVED FOR THE CHRISTENING OF KING JAMES' SON, HENRY.

the Bonnet

BONNET ONLY

REQUIREMENTS

Fabric & Lace

White cotton tulle
20cm x 145cm wide (8" x 57")
for all sizes

White cotton lace edging
1.6m x 8mm wide (1yd 27" x ⁵/₁₆")

White cotton lace beading
40cm x 12mm wide (15 ³/₄" x ¹/₂")

White cotton lace insertion
1.6m x 8mm wide (1yd 27" x ⁵/₁₆")

Notions

Bridal white double sided satin ribbon
1.2m x 5mm wide (1yd 11 ¹/₄" x ³/₁₆")

White cotton heirloom machine sewing thread

Fine water-soluble fabric marker

No. 10 crewel needle

No. 10 straw needle

Threads & Ribbons

YLI silk ribbon 7mm (⁵/₁₆") wide
A = no. 3 bridal white
55cm (21 ⁵/₈")

DMC stranded cotton
B = blanc

Anchor stranded silk
C = 926 cream

PATTERN & CUTTING OUT

See the liftout pattern sheet for the pattern and cutting layout.

Cut out all pieces following the instructions on the liftout pattern sheet.

PREPARATION FOR EMBROIDERY

See the liftout pattern sheet for the embroidery design.

Assemble the bonnet following the instructions on page 118.

Place clear plastic film over the embroidery design on the master pattern, or alternatively, trace the embroidery design onto white paper with a black pen.

Turn the bonnet inside out and centre the crown over the embroidery design. Mark the position of each flower in the same manner as before.

EMBROIDERY

Make five gathered ribbon flowers in the same manner as those on the yoke. Attach three to the centre of the crown in a cluster. Embroider three bullion buds between the ribbon flowers.

Position the remaining ribbon flowers on the bonnet brim, one at each end. When securing them to the bonnet, ensure the thread goes through all layers including the ribbon ties.

CONSTRUCTION

See page 118.

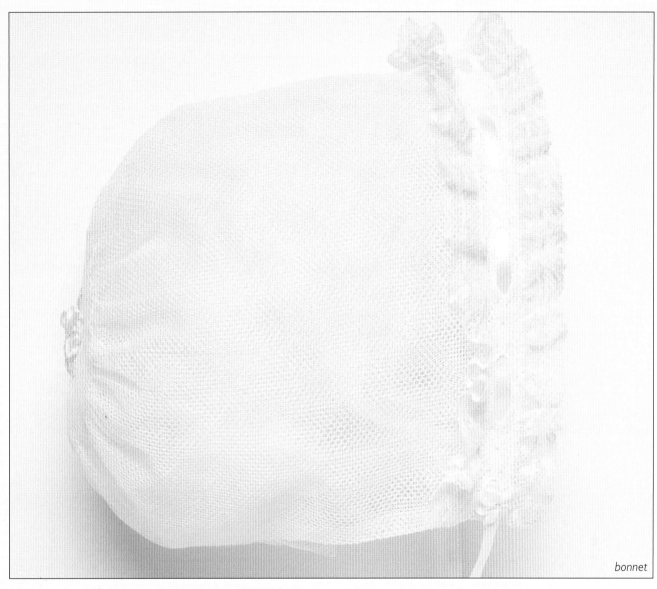

bonnet

crown embroidery

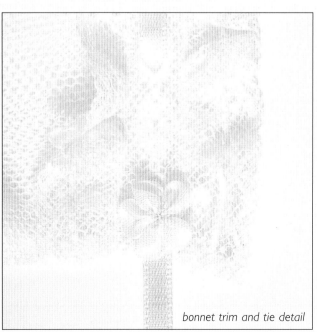

bonnet trim and tie detail

gown front

gown back

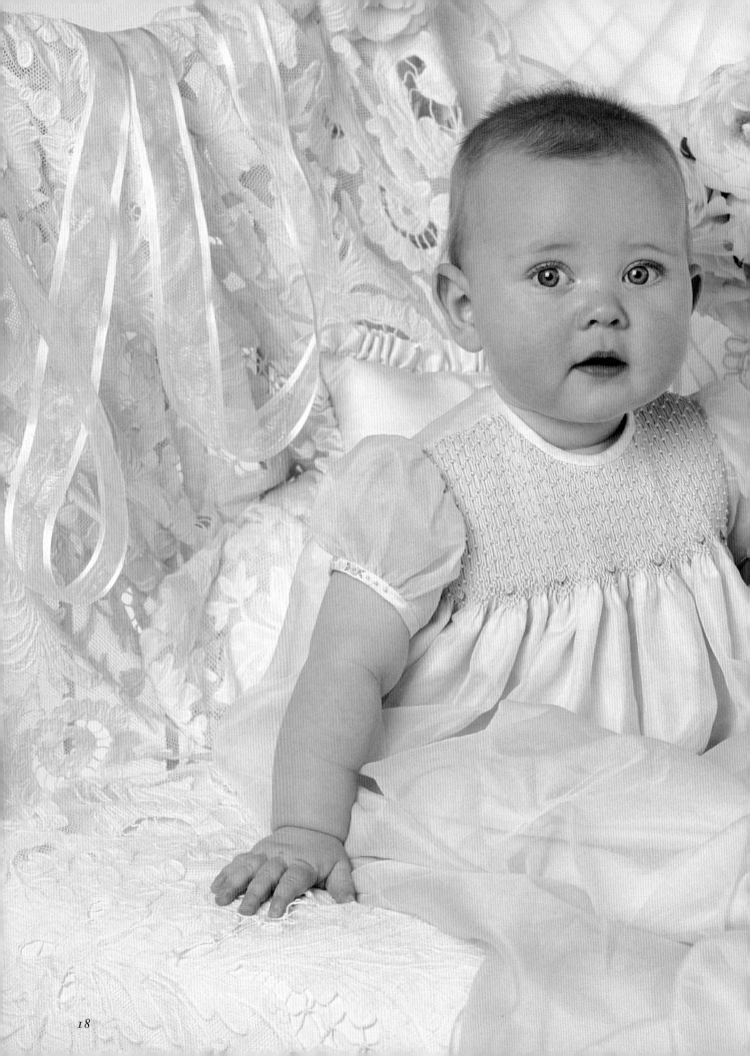

*Softest blush pink silk has been lovingly stitched to create this enchanting gown.
The smocked bodice is sprinkled with tiny pearl beads and is finished
at the lower edge with delicate pink rosebuds.
Roses, rosebuds and flowing ribbons encircle the gently scalloped hem.*

Sizes 3, 6 & 12 months

GOWN

REQUIREMENTS

Fabric

Pale pink silk organza
2.2m x 114cm wide
(2yd 14 ⁵/₈" x 45") for all sizes

Pale pink silk dupion
2.6m x 114cm wide
(2yd 30 ³/₈" x 45") for all sizes

Notions

7 pearl buttons 11mm (³/₈") wide

1 small clear snap fastener

Fine water-soluble fabric marker

Small embroidery hoop

No. 9 straw needle

Threads & Beads

1 string of ivory pearl beads
2mm (¹/₁₆") wide

Madeira stranded silk
A = 0815 ultra light shell pink
B = 1510 light green-grey

Anchor stranded cotton
C = 893 very light shell pink

PATTERN & CUTTING OUT

*See the liftout pattern sheet for the
pattern and cutting layouts.*

Front overskirt: cut one,
96.5cm x 114cm wide (38" x 45")
from the silk organza for all sizes.

Front underskirt: cut one,
101.5cm x 114cm wide (40" x 45")
from the silk dupion for all sizes.

Cut out all other pieces following the
instructions on the liftout pattern sheet.

PREPARATION & PLEATING

Place the two front skirts together,
ensuring the wrong side of the organza
is against the right side of the silk
dupion. Tack the two layers together
with a row of stitches approximately

5mm (³/₁₆") from the top raw edge.
Work another four rows of tacking,
placing each row approximately 2.5cm
(1") from the previous row *(diag 1)*.

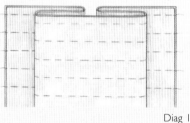

Diag 1

Pleat fourteen full space rows (including
one holding row at the bottom) with
the first row 1cm (³/₈") from the top
raw edge. Remove the tacking and
unpick the pleats on both sides for
3.5cm (1³/₈"). Tie off the pleating
threads to fit the front blocking guide.

Count the pleats and mark the centre
valley. Place the blocking guide over
the pleated fabric, aligning the centre
valley with the centre of the guide.
Mark the armhole and neck shaping
onto the fabric with the fabric marker.

SMOCKING

Note: Small pearl beads are added to the over and under cables in each row. Only add the pearls to the stitches that fall within the marked bodice area.

Row 1 - 1 ¹/₂. Begin on the centre two pleats on row 1 with an over cable. Work two-step trellis down to row 1 ¹/₂, slip a bead onto the needle, work an under cable then two-step trellis up to row 1. Continue working two-step trellis to the end of the row adding beads to the cables. Turn the fabric upside down, return to the centre and complete the row.

Rows 2 - 11 ¹/₂. Following the graph, work ten rows of two-step trellis, adding beads to the under and over cables.

Row 11 ¹/₂ - 12 ¹/₂. Begin at the centre two pleats on row 12 with an under cable. Work two-step trellis up to row 11 ¹/₂. Take the needle through the bead of the previous row and work five-step trellis down to row 12 ¹/₂. Add a bead to the needle, work an under cable and then five-step trellis up to row 11 ¹/₂. Maintaining the pattern, continue to the end of the row. Turn the fabric upside down, return to the centre and complete the row.

Row 12 - 13. Repeat the previous row, adding a bead to both the under and over cables.

PREPARATION FOR EMBROIDERY

See the liftout pattern sheet for the embroidery designs.

Remove the pleating threads and block the smocking to fit the front blocking guide.

STITCHES & TECHNIQUES USED

BEADED TWO-STEP TRELLIS

BEADED FIVE-STEP TRELLIS

BULLION KNOT

DETACHED CHAIN

SHADOW WORK -
DOUBLE BACK STITCH

STRAIGHT STITCH

Assemble the gown following the instructions on pages 119 - 122.

Using the fabric marker, mark the centre of each sleeve binding with a dot.

Trace the bow design onto a piece of paper. Place the design under the organza skirt, positioning it so the centre of the bow knot is 12mm (¹/₂") above the peak of one scallop. Lightly trace the design lines with the fabric marker. Repeat at the peak of each scallop.

At the centre of one scallop, measure up 1cm (³/₈") from the silk dupion and mark the position with a dot. Repeat at the centre of each scallop.

EMBROIDERY

Embroidery on the smocking

Using the darkest shade of pink and following the graph for placement, work two horizontal bullion knots across the centre two pleats in each heart shape to form the centres of the rosebuds. Change to the lighter pink thread and work three overlapping bullion knots for the petals. Add two detached chain leaves to each rosebud.

Embroidery on the hemline

Shadow work the bows using the lighter pink thread and double back stitch. Work a rosebud over each bow knot in the same manner as those on the smocking. Add three detached chain leaves below each bud. Secure one pearl bead above the rose and two below. Link each bead to the rosebud with a straight stitch.

Attach three evenly spaced beads in a vertical line below the centre of each peak. Position the beads approximately 6mm (¹/₄") apart. Attach a pearl bead to the lowest fold in each ribbon tie.

Work a bullion rose at the marked position above the centre of one scallop. Add two detached chain leaves on each side of the rose and then a single pearl bead.

Embroidery on the sleeve bindings

Work a bullion rose at the centre of one sleeve binding. Add two detached chain leaves to each side of the rose. Secure three evenly spaced pearl beads to each side of the rose, positioning them approximately 6mm (¹/₄") apart. Repeat on the remaining sleeve binding.

CONSTRUCTION

See pages 119 - 122.

The finished length of the gown from the centre back neckline to the hemline is 95cm (37 3/8") for all sizes.

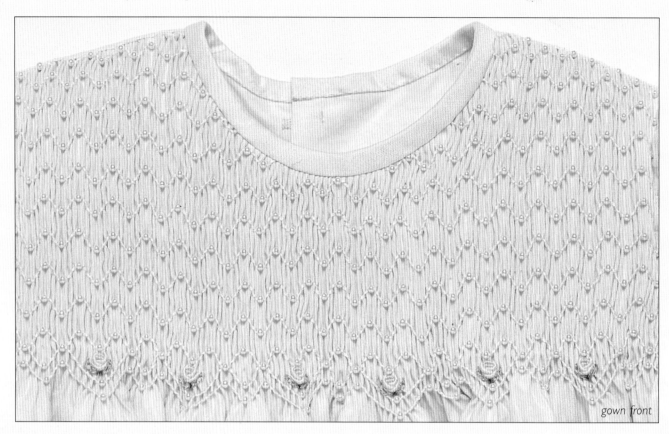

gown front

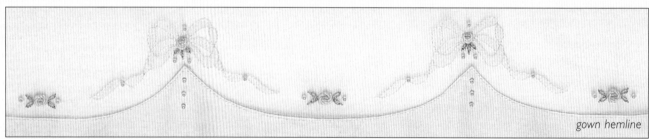

gown hemline

sleeve binding

SMOCKING & EMBROIDERY KEY

All smocking and embroidery is worked with two strands of thread unless otherwise specified.

Smocking

Rows 1 - 11 1/2 = A
(beaded two-step trellis)

Rows 11 1/2 - 13 = A
(beaded two-step/five-step trellis combination)

Embroidery

Rosebuds

Centre = C
(2 bullion knots, 8 wraps)

Middle petals = A
(2 bullion knots, 12 wraps)

Lowest petal = A
(1 bullion knot, 16 wraps)

Roses

Centre = C
(2 bullion knots, 10 wraps)

Petals = A (5 - 6 bullion knots, 10 wraps)

Leaves = B
(1 strand, detached chain)

Bows = A
(1 strand, shadow work)

WHEN YOU CHRISTEN THE BAIRN,
YOU SHOULD KNOW WHAT TO CALL IT.

SCOTTISH PROVERB

PATTERN REPEAT

gown front

~ STARDUST ~

BABIES ARE BITS OF STARDUST BLOWN FROM THE HAND OF GOD.

LARRY BARRETTO

Dainty hand stitched scallops finish the neckline, sleeves and lower edge
of this sweet little gown. Delicate sprays of tiny flowers decorate the front
and the sleeves are finished with tiny eyelets threaded with soft satin ribbons.

Sizes 3, 6 & 12 months

GOWN, PETTICOAT & BONNET

REQUIREMENTS

Fabric

White cotton voile

Size 3 months: 1.7m x 112cm wide
(1yd 31" x 44")

Size 6 months: 1.8m x 112cm wide
(1yd 35" x 44")

Size 12 months: 1.9m x 112cm wide
(2yd 2 3/4" x 44")

Notions

8 pearl buttons 7mm (5/16") wide

White double-sided satin ribbon
1m x 7mm wide (1yd 3 3/8" x 5/16")

White double-sided satin ribbon
1.5m x 15mm wide (1yd 23" x 5/8")

30cm (11 3/4") narrow white entredeux

Water-soluble fabric stabilizer

Fine water-soluble fabric marker

Small embroidery hoop

Dressmaker's awl

No. 10 sharp needle

Thread

DMC stranded cotton

A = blanc

EMBROIDERY KEY

All embroidery is worked with
one strand of thread.

Scallops = A (blanket stitch)

Fronds

Stems = A (stem stitch)

Leaves = A (granitos)

Flowers

Petals = A
(granitos or detached chain)

Centre = A
(French knot, 2 wraps, or none)

Small buds = A
(French knot, 1 - 2 wraps)

Eyelets on sleeves = A

STITCHES & TECHNIQUES USED

ATTACHING ENTREDEUX TO FLAT FABRIC, BLANKET STITCH, BUTTONHOLE STITCH

DETACHED CHAIN, EYELET, FRENCH KNOT, GRANITOS, RIBBON ROSETTE, STEM STITCH

by LORRAINE BERGERON

the Gown

GOWN ONLY

REQUIREMENTS

Fabric

White cotton voile

Size 3 months: 1m x 112cm wide (1yd 3 3/8" x 44")

Size 6 months: 1.1m x 112cm wide (1yd 7 1/4" x 44")

Size 12 months: 1.2m x 112cm wide (2yd 11 1/4" x 44")

Notions

5 pearl buttons 7mm (5/16") wide

White double-sided satin ribbon 1m x 7mm wide (1yd 3 3/8" x 5/16")

Water-soluble fabric stabilizer

Fine water-soluble fabric marker

Small embroidery hoop

Dressmaker's awl

No. 10 sharp needle

Thread

DMC stranded cotton

A = blanc

PATTERN & CUTTING OUT

See the liftout pattern sheet for the pattern and cutting layouts.

Cut out all pieces following the instructions on the liftout pattern sheet.

PREPARATION FOR EMBROIDERY

See the liftout pattern sheet for the embroidery designs.

Working the scallops

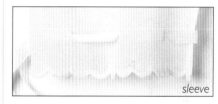

Diag 1

Using fine French seams, stitch the front to the back at the shoulders and sides *(diag 1)*. Complete the button bands following the instructions on page 122.

Press and spray starch the fabric. Allow it to cool. Place the fabric over the pattern pieces and mark the scallop lines around the neckline, sleeves and lower edge using the fabric marker.

Placing water-soluble fabric stabilizer behind the area to be stitched and using a machine scallop stitch approximately 12mm (1/2") long, stitch along the marked large scallops around the lower edge of the gown.

Work machine scallops around the neckline and across the lower edge of each sleeve in the same manner. Using small sharp scissors, carefully cut along the scallops, taking care not to cut the stitching. Rinse to remove the fabric stabilizer. Leave until dry and press.

Transferring the embroidery designs

Aligning stitchlines, position the front of the gown over the front pattern piece. Using the fabric marker, trace the five embroidery motifs down the centre front and the four motifs along the hemline.

Place each sleeve over the sleeve pattern piece and transfer the positions of the eyelets with the fabric marker.

EMBROIDERY

Scallops

Using one strand of thread, embroider over all machine stitched scallops in blanket stitch.

Embroidery on the front

Embroider the stems of the fronds in stem stitch. Work a granitos of approximately four straight stitches for each leaf. Stitch each flower with 4 to 5 petals, working a granitos for each one. Add a two-wrap French knot to the centre of each flower and then work tiny French knot buds. Use two wraps for the knots closest to the flowers and one wrap for the farthest buds.

Embroidery on the sleeves

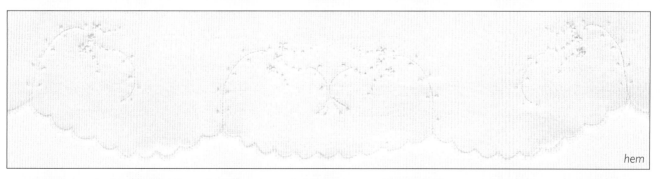

sleeve

Use the dressmaker's awl to pierce the fabric at each marked position for the eyelets. Complete each eyelet following the step-by-step instructions on page 90.

CONSTRUCTION

See page 122.

hem

The finished length of the gown from the centre back neckline to the hemline is

Size 3 months: 62cm (24 3/8") Size 6 months: 67cm (26 3/8") Size 12 months: 72cm (28 3/8")

the Petticoat

petticoat

PETTICOAT ONLY

REQUIREMENTS

Fabric

White cotton voile

Size 3 months: 80cm x 112cm wide
(31 1/2" x 44")
Size 6 months: 90cm x 112cm wide
(35 1/2" x 44")
Size 12 months: 1m x 112cm wide
(1yd 3 3/8" x 44")

Notions

3 pearl buttons 7mm (5/16") wide
Water-soluble fabric stabilizer
Fine water-soluble fabric marker
No. 10 sharp needle

Thread

DMC stranded cotton
A = blanc

PATTERN & CUTTING OUT

See the liftout pattern sheet for the pattern and cutting layouts.

Cut out all pieces following the instructions on the liftout pattern sheet.

PREPARATION FOR EMBROIDERY

See the liftout pattern sheet for the embroidery designs.

Working the scallops

Using fine French seams, stitch the front to the back at the shoulders. Complete the button bands following the instructions on page 123.

Press and spray starch the fabric. Allow it to cool. Place the fabric over the pattern pieces and mark the scallop lines around the neckline and armholes using the fabric marker.

Placing water-soluble fabric stabilizer behind the area to be stitched and using a machine scallop stitch approximately 12mm (1/2") long, stitch around the neckline and armholes. Using small sharp scissors, carefully cut along the scallops, taking care not to cut the stitching. Stitch the side seams using fine French seams. Prepare, stitch and cut out the machine scallops around the lower edge in the same manner.

Rinse to remove the fabric stabilizer. Leave until dry and press.

Transferring the embroidery design

Fold the petticoat in half to find the centre front. Mark with a pin. Aligning the pin with the placement marks on the embroidery design, place the petticoat over the design. Trace with the fabric marker.

EMBROIDERY

Scallops

Embroider over the machine stitched scallops in the same manner as the gown.

Embroidery on the front

Stitch the embroidery motif below the neckline in a similar manner to the embroidery on the gown, omitting the centres from the flowers. Use two wraps for the French knot buds near the flowers and one wrap for the buds at the end of the frond.

CONSTRUCTION

See page 123.

the Bonnet

crown embroidery

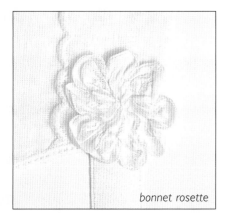

bonnet rosette

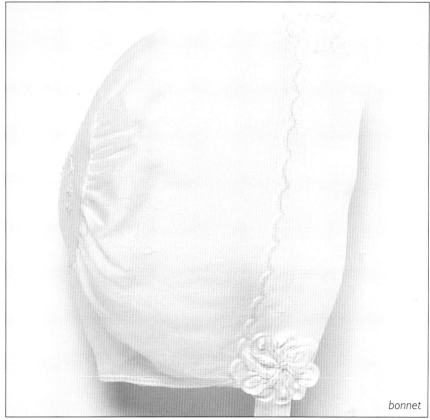

bonnet

BONNET ONLY

REQUIREMENTS

Fabric

White cotton voile
30cm x 70cm wide (11 ³/4" x 27 ¹/2")
for all sizes

Notions

White double-sided satin ribbon
1.5m x 15mm wide (1yd 23" x ⁵/8")

30cm (11 ³/4") narrow white entredeux

Water-soluble fabric stabilizer

Fine water-soluble fabric marker

Small embroidery hoop

No. 10 sharp needle

Thread

DMC stranded cotton

A = blanc

PATTERN & CUTTING OUT

*See the liftout pattern sheet for the
pattern and cutting layouts.*

Cut out all pieces following the
instructions on the liftout pattern sheet.

PREPARATION FOR EMBROIDERY

Working the scallops

Press and spray starch the fabric. Allow
it to cool. Place the bonnet over the
pattern piece and mark the scallop line
along the brim using the fabric marker.

With the wrong side of the bonnet
uppermost, place water-soluble fabric
stabilizer behind the area to be
stitched. Using a machine scallop
stitch approximately 12mm (¹/2")
long, work machine scallops across
the bonnet turnback. Using small
sharp scissors, carefully cut along the
scallops, taking care not to cut the
stitching. Rinse to remove the fabric
stabilizer. Leave until dry and press.

Transferring the embroidery motifs

With the right side uppermost, position

the crown over the crown pattern
piece. Using the fabric marker, trace
the design.

Repeat the procedure with the
turnback, ensuring the wrong side of
the bonnet is uppermost.

EMBROIDERY

Scallops

Embroider over the machine stitched
scallops in the same manner as the
gown.

Embroidery motifs

Stitch the embroidery motif on the
turnback in the same manner as the
top embroidery design on the gown.
Embroider the motif on the crown in a
similar manner but use detached
chains, rather than granitos, for the
petals of the flowers.

CONSTRUCTION

See pages 123 - 124.

gown front

gown back

An ivory silk romper in soft crêpe de chine featuring gentle bodice tucks,

entredeux and rows of elegant embroidery. A piped collar completes the neckline

and the sleeves and legs are finished with piped bands.

Sizes 3, 6 and 12 months

REQUIREMENTS

Fabric

Ivory silk crêpe de chine
1.3m x 112cm wide (1yd 15 ¼" x 44")
for all sizes

Notions

10 pearl buttons 11mm (³/₈") wide

2.3m (2yd 18 ½") narrow ivory
entredeux

Lightweight woven fusible interfacing
30cm x 45cm wide (11³/₄" x 17³/₄")

1.3m (1yd 15 ¼") fine piping cord

Fine water-soluble fabric marker

No. 8 crewel needle

Thread

Anchor Marlitt stranded rayon
A = 1034 ivory

STITCHES & TECHNIQUES USED

RUSSIAN CHAIN STITCH
VARIATION

ATTACHING ENTREDEUX
TO FLAT FABRIC

PATTERN & CUTTING OUT

See the liftout pattern sheet for the pattern and cutting layout.

Cut a 25cm x 55cm wide (10" x 21⁵/₈") rectangle from the crêpe de chine for the front bodice. The bodice will be cut to shape after the centre front pleat, tucks, entredeux and embroidery have been stitched.

Cut out all other pieces following the instructions on the liftout pattern sheet.

EMBROIDERY KEY

All embroidery is worked with one strand of thread.

Embroidery = A
(Russian chain stitch variation)

PREPARATION FOR EMBROIDERY

Centre front pleat and tucks

With wrong sides together, fold the rectangle in half widthwise. Clip the fold at the upper and lower edges to mark the centre front. Stitch through both layers 3.5cm (1 ¼") from the fold. Press to form a box pleat, aligning the clipped points with the seam at the back. Stitch two 1cm (³/₈") wide tucks on each side of the box pleat and press (see diag 1).

Press and stitch one tuck before pressing and stitching the next tuck. When stitching, use the fold of the previous tuck as a guide for stitching.

Entredeux

Cut off the excess fabric on the left hand side of the panel, leaving 1cm (³/₈") of fabric extending past the fold of the last tuck (diag 1).

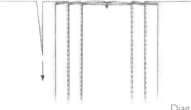

Diag 1

Cut two pieces of entredeux, each 25cm (10") long. Trim the headings to 1cm (³/₈") if necessary.

With right sides together and matching raw edges, pin and stitch one piece of entredeux to the panel, placing the stitching as close as possible to the embroidered holes of the entredeux (diag 2).

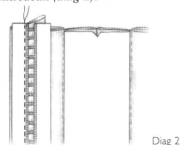

Diag 2

Trim the seam allowance to 2 - 3mm (¹/₈"). Roll and whip the seam using a close zigzag stitch wide enough to cover the previous straight stitching on

front

one side and to just miss the raw edge of the fabric on the other (diag 3).

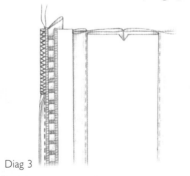

Diag 3

Press the entredeux away from the fabric and the seam towards the tuck. Reattach the excess fabric to the remaining edge of the entredeux using the same method.

Leaving 3.5cm (1 ³/₈") of fabric past the entredeux, cut away the excess fabric on the left hand side of the panel again. Insert the second length of entredeux in the same manner as before.

Repeat on the right hand side of the panel to create a mirror image of the left hand side (diag 4).

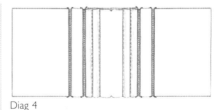

Diag 4

Embroidery placement marks

Using the fabric marker, rule a line down the centre of the narrow band of fabric between the rows of entredeux on the left hand side. Rule lines approximately 3mm (¹/₈") away on both sides of this centre line. Beginning 12mm (¹/₂") from the lower edge, mark the centre line with dots 5mm (³/₁₆") apart.

Repeat on the other side of the panel.

EMBROIDERY

Beginning at the top and working downwards, embroider Russian chain stitch variation down the centre of each narrow band of fabric following the step-by-step instructions on page 91.

CONSTRUCTION

See pages 124 - 127.

romper front

romper back

Ivory lace encircles the yoke and sleeves of this beautiful bishop gown.
Stitched in shades of rich cream, the smocking is highlighted with plump roses
and daisies embroidered in glowing silk thread.

Sizes 3, 6 and 12 months

REQUIREMENTS

Fabric & Lace

Rice cotton batiste
2.25m x 112cm wide
(2yd 16 5/8" x 44") for all sizes

Ivory cotton lace edging (for neck frill)
2.5m x 35mm wide
(2yd 26 1/2" x 1 3/8")

Ivory cotton lace edging (for sleeves)
1.2m x 20mm wide
(1yd 11 1/4" x 3/4") for all sizes

Ivory cotton lace insertion (for sleeves)
1.2m x 25mm wide
(1yd 11 1/4" x 1") for all sizes

Notions

5 shell buttons 11mm (7/16") wide
1 shell button 7mm (5/16") wide
Fine water-soluble fabric marker
No. 7 crewel needle
No. 3 straw needle

Threads

Au Ver à Soie, Soie d'Alger
A = mode (2 skeins)
B = F1 dark cream (2 skeins)

C = 1731 ice blue
D = 2132 light olive green
E = 2241 light old gold
F = 2941 rose pink
G = 3043 ultra light shell pink
(2 skeins)

STITCHES & TECHNIQUES USED

CABLE STITCH

TRELLIS-WAVE COMBINATION

TRELLIS-WAVE-STEM-OUTLINE
COMBINATION

BULLION KNOT

BULLION LOOP

FLY STITCH

FRENCH KNOT

ATTACHING FLAT LACE
TO FLAT FABRIC

PATTERN & CUTTING OUT

See the liftout pattern sheet for the
pattern and cutting layout.

Front: cut one from the rice batiste

Size 3 months:
92cm x 73cm wide (36 1/4" x 28 3/4")

Size 6 months:
92cm x 75cm wide (36 1/4" x 29 1/2")

Size 12 months:
92cm x 77cm wide (36 1/4" x 30 1/4")

Back: cut two from the rice batiste, each

Size 3 months:
92cm x 38cm wide (36 1/4" x 15")

Size 6 months:
92cm x 40cm wide (36 1/4" x 15 3/4")

Size 12 months:
92cm x 42cm wide (36 1/4" x 16 1/2")

Sleeves: cut two from the rice
batiste, each

Size 3 months:
20.5cm x 38cm wide (8" x 15")

Size 6 months:
22cm x 40cm wide (8 5/8" x 15 3/4")

Size 12 months:
23.5cm x 42cm wide (9 1/4" x 16 1/2")

by SUSAN O'CONNOR

Using the armhole cutting guide and aligning the placement marks on the guide with the raw edges of the fabric, transfer the armhole shape to both top corners of the front. Cut away the excess fabric *(diag 1)*.

Diag 1

Transfer and cut out the armhole shape from one top corner on each back piece, ensuring you have a right and a left back *(diag 2)*.

Diag 2

Cut out the armhole shaping from each sleeve in the same manner as the front. Rule a line 4.5cm (1 3/4") up from the lower edge on each sleeve. Rule another line 2cm (3/4") above.

PREPARATION & PLEATING

See the liftout pattern sheet for the bishop blocking guide.

Sleeves

Cut a piece of lace insertion and a piece of narrow lace edging to fit the lower edge of the sleeve.

Attach the lace insertion between the marked lines and the lace edging to the lower edge *(diag 3)*.

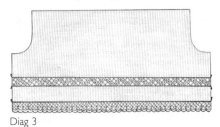
Diag 3

Using long threads, pleat five half space rows (including two holding rows), centering the rows between the lace edging and lace insertion on the lower section of the sleeves.

Unpick the pleating threads for 4cm (1 1/2") at each end and flatten out the pleats. After the neckline has been pleated and the threads tied off, pull up the pleating threads in the sleeves and tie them off so the sleeve measures approximately 18cm (7") wide.

Neckline

Stitch the sleeves to the front and backs following the diagram below *(diag 4)*.

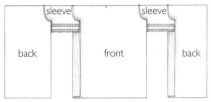
Diag 4

Trim the seams to 4mm (3/16") and neaten with a machine zigzag or overlock stitch. Press the seams to one side.

Measure down 6cm (2 3/8") from the raw edge of the neckline. Using the fabric marker, rule a line across the entire gown at this measurement.

Position the wide lace edging onto the right side of the gown, aligning the lace heading with the ruled line. Pin in place. Using a machine straight stitch, stitch along the lace heading *(diag 5)*.

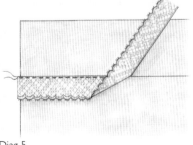
Diag 5

Tack along the lower edge of the lace.

Pleat fifteen half space rows (including two holding rows) with the eleventh pleating thread aligned with the lace heading (row 10 on the graph). Pleat slowly over the seams.

Unpick the pleating threads for 7.5cm (3") at each back opening edge. Remove the tacking from the lower edge of the lace. Place the pleated neckline over the bishop blocking guide and match centre front, centre backs and sleeve seams with the marks on the guide. Fan out the pleats to fit the guide and pin in place. Tie off the pleating threads except for the top holding row.

SMOCKING

Work all smocking with the crewel needle.

Neckline

Count the pleats and mark the centre valley.

Row 1 - 3. Using the dark cream thread, begin on the centre two pleats on row 2 with an over cable. Work wave down to row 3, under cable. Work six more waves, under cable, three-step trellis up to row 1, over cable, three-step trellis down to row 3, under cable, seven waves. Continue in this manner to the end of the row. Turn the fabric upside down, return to the centre and complete the row.

Rows 2 - 5. Change to the mode thread. Repeat the previous row twice.

Row 4 - 6. Repeat row 1 - 3.

Row 6 - 8. Work a mirror image of the previous row.

Row 7 - 10. Begin on the centre two pleats on row 7 with an over cable. Work wave down to row 8, ten outline stitches, six-step trellis down to row 10, under cable, six-step trellis up to row 8, ten stem stitches, wave up to row 7. Continue to the end of the row in the same manner. Turn the fabric upside down, return to the centre and complete the row.

Row 10 - 13. Work a mirror image of the previous row

Backsmocking

The backsmocking is worked on the wrong side of the pleats and only the tip of each pleat is picked up with the needle.

Top holding row. Beginning on the left hand side, work stem stitch across the row.

Row 10. Beginning on the left hand side, work cable across the row.

Sleeves

Count the pleats and mark the centre valley.

Row 1 - 2. Using the dark cream thread, begin on the centre two pleats on row 1 with an over cable. Work wave down to row 2, under cable, wave up to row 1. Continue in this manner to the end of the row. Turn the fabric upside down, return to the centre and complete the row.

Row 2 - 3. Repeat the previous row.

PREPARATION FOR EMBROIDERY

Remove the pleating threads from the neckline, except for the top holding row. Remove all the pleating threads from the sleeves.

EMBROIDERY

Neckline

Along row 6, embroider a bullion rosebud in each trellis diamond. Work a bullion loop for the centre and then stitch two overlapping bullion knots around the lower half for the petals. Surround the rosebud with a fly stitch for the sepals and stem.

Each hexagonal shape between rows 8 and 12 is encrusted with flowers. Using the photograph as a guide, embroider the three large bullion roses first. Work a small bullion rose at each end of the hexagonal shape. Stitch two fly stitches around each rose for sepals.

Work the two daisies next, stitching four bullion loops for the petals and a French knot for the centre of each one. Anchor each loop near the top. Stitch a pair of leaves alongside each daisy. For each leaf, work two bullion knots side by side that use the same holes in the fabric.

Finally, add clusters of blue and cream French knots for tiny buds.

Sleeves

Embroider a single bullion rose at the centre of the smocking on each sleeve. Add a fly stitch around the rose and two bullion leaves just below it, working them in the same manner as those on the neckline. Stitch a cluster of five blue French knots below the leaves.

CONSTRUCTION

See pages 127 - 128.

SMOCKING & EMBROIDERY KEY

All smocking and embroidery is worked with three strands of thread unless otherwise specified.

Smocking on neckline

Row 1 - 3 = B (three-step trellis/wave combination)

Rows 2 - 5 = A (three-step trellis/wave combination)

Rows 4 - 8 = B (three-step trellis/wave combination)

Rows 7 - 13 = B (six-step trellis/stem stitch /wave/outline stitch combination)

Backsmocking

Top holding row = B (2 strands, stem stitch)

Row 10 = B (2 strands, cable stitch)

Smocking on sleeves

Rows 1 - 3 = B (wave stitch)

Embroidery on neckline

Rosebuds in diamonds

Centre = G (1 bullion loop, 10 wraps)

Petals = A (2 bullion knots, 10 wraps)

Sepals and stem = D (fly stitch)

Large roses

Centre = F (1 bullion loop, 10 wraps)

Middle petals = G 6 bullion knots, 10 wraps)

Outer petals = A (3 bullion knots, 12 wraps)

Sepals = D (fly stitch)

Small roses

Centre = F (1 bullion loop, 10 wraps)

Middle petals = G (2 bullion knots, 10 wraps)

Outer petals = A (1 bullion knot, 12 wraps)

Sepals = D (fly stitch)

Daisies

Centre = E (French knot, 2 wraps)

Petals = A (4 bullion loops, 15 wraps)

Leaves = D (2 bullion knots, 7 wraps)

Tiny buds = B and C (French knot, 2 wraps)

Embroidery on sleeves

Rose

Centre = F (1 bullion loop, 10 wraps)

Middle petals = G (6 bullion knots, 10 wraps)

Outer petals = A (3 bullion knots, 12 wraps)

Sepals = D (fly stitch)

Leaves = D (2 bullion knots, 7 wraps)

Tiny buds = C (French knot, 2 wraps)

The finished length of the gown from the centre back neckline to the hemline is 85cm (33 ½") for all sizes.

neckline

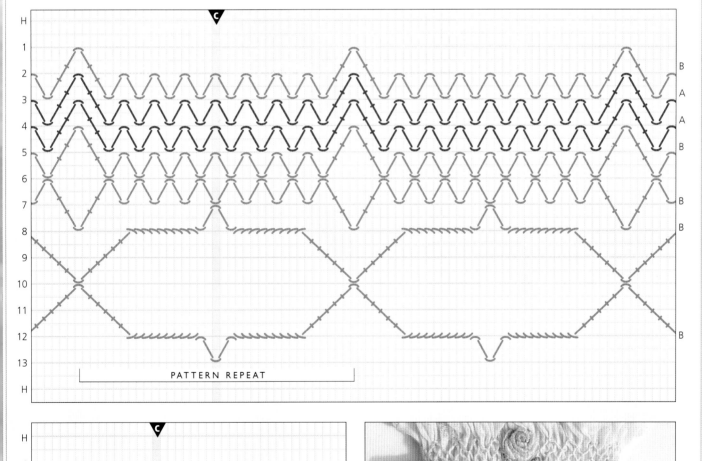

PATTERN REPEAT

sleeve

gown front

gown back

A truly sumptuous smocked gown of ivory silk organza lavishly trimmed with beaded tucks and rows of exquisite lace. Matching lace trims the silk bonnet and is used to create the delicate bolero.

Sizes 3, 6 & 12 months

GOWN, BOLERO & BONNET

REQUIREMENTS

Fabric & Lace

Ivory silk organza
3.2m x 130cm wide (3yd 18" x 51")
for all sizes

Ivory Swiss batiste
2m x 130cm wide (2yd 6 3/4" x 51")
for all sizes

Ivory lace edging
4.8m x 20mm wide (5yd 9" x 3/4")
for all sizes

Ivory lace edging
2.7m x 40mm wide
(2yd 34 1/4" x 1 1/2") for all sizes

Ivory lace beading
12.1m x 18mm wide
(13yd 8" x 11/16") for all sizes

Ivory lace insertion (floral)
25m x 18mm wide
(27yd 12" x 11/16") for all sizes

Ivory lace insertion (diamonds)
7m x 18mm wide
(7yd 23 5/8" x 11/16") for all sizes

Ivory entredeux beading
40cm x 11mm wide (15 3/4" x 7/16")
for all sizes

Narrow ivory entredeux
75cm (29 1/2") for all sizes

Notions

6 shell heart buttons 11mm (7/16") wide

1 small clear snap fastener

YLI no. 01 antique white silk ribbon
12.1m x 2mm wide (13yd 8" x 3/32")

Ivory silk satin ribbon 50cm x 3mm
wide (19 3/4" x 1/8")

Ivory silk satin ribbon 90cm x 6mm
wide (35 1/2" x 1/4")

Ivory organdie ribbon 1.4m x 38mm
wide (1yd 19" x 1 1/2")

Fine water-soluble fabric marker

No. 9 straw needle

Threads & Beads

Kanagawa 1000 denier silk floss
A = 00 white

Mill Hill Magnifica glass beads
B = 10046 white opal

STITCHES & TECHNIQUES USED

BEADING

RUNNING STITCH

TWO-STEP WAVE/CABLE COMBINATION

BEADING ON SMOCKING

FOUR-STEP WAVE/CABLE COMBINATION

CABLE STITCH

ATTACHING FLAT LACE TO FLAT LACE

ATTACHING FLAT LACE TO FLAT FABRIC

ATTACHING FLAT LACE TO ENTREDEUX

ATTACHING GATHERED FABRIC TO ENTREDEUX

ATTACHING GATHERED LACE TO ENTREDEUX

MITRED LACE

MACHINE PIN STITCH

by GAIL DOANE

REQUIREMENTS

Fabric & Lace

Ivory silk organza
2.6m x 130cm wide
(2yd 30 3/8" x 51") for all sizes

Ivory Swiss batiste
2m x 130cm wide (2yd 6 3/4" x 51")
for all sizes

Ivory lace edging
2m x 20mm wide (2yd 6 3/4" x 3/4")
for all sizes

Ivory lace edging
2.7m x 40mm wide
(2yd 34 1/4" x 1 1/2") for all sizes

Ivory lace beading
8.3m x 18mm wide (9yd 3" x 11/16")
for all sizes

Ivory lace insertion (floral)
16.3m x 18mm wide
(17yd 30" x 11/16") for all sizes

Notions

3 shell heart buttons 11mm (7/16") wide

YLI no. 01 antique white silk ribbon
8.3m x 2mm wide (9yd 3" x 3/32")

Fine water-soluble fabric marker

No. 9 straw needle

Threads & Beads

Kanagawa 1000 denier silk floss
A = 00 white

Mill Hill Magnifica glass beads
B = 10046 white opal

PATTERN & CUTTING OUT

See the liftout pattern sheet for the
pattern and cutting layouts.

Front overskirt: cut one from the
silk organza, 119cm x 130cm wide
(46 3/4" x 51") for all sizes.

Front underskirt: cut one from the
Swiss batiste, 87cm x 130cm wide
(34 1/8" x 51") for all sizes.

Cut out all other pieces following the
instructions on the liftout pattern
sheet.

PREPARATION & PLEATING

Place the two front skirts together,
ensuring the wrong side of the
organza is against the right side of the
batiste. Tack the two layers together
with a row of stitches approximately
5mm (3/16") from the top raw edge.
Work another seven rows of tacking,
placing each row approximately
2.5cm (1") from the previous row
(diag 1).

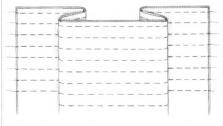

Diag 1

Pleat twenty full space rows (including
one holding row at the bottom) with
the first row 1cm (3/8") from the top
raw edge. Remove the tacking and
unpick the pleats on both sides for
1cm (3/8"). Tie off the pleating threads
to fit the front blocking guide.

Mark the armhole and neck shaping
onto the fabric with the fabric marker.

SMOCKING

Note: Small beads are added to the
cable stitches in each row. Only add
the beads to the stitches that fall
within the marked bodice area.

Count the pleats and mark the centre
valley.

Row 1 - 1 1/2. Begin on the centre two
pleats on row 1 1/2 with an under cable.
Work wave up to row 1 1/4, slip a bead
onto the needle, cable, wave up to row
1, slip a bead onto the needle, over
cable, wave down to row 1 1/4, slip a
bead onto the needle, cable, wave
down to row 1 1/2, slip a bead onto the
needle. Continue working the two-step
wave cable combination to the end of
the row adding beads to the cables.
Turn the fabric upside down, return to
the centre and complete the row.

Row 1 1/2 - 2. Bring the thread to the
front on row 2 between the fourth and
fifth pleats to the left of the centre
valley. Take the needle through the
pleat on the left, slip a bead onto the
needle and work an under cable on
row 2. Work wave up to row 1 3/4, slip
a bead onto the needle, cable, wave up
to row 1 1/2, over cable, wave down to
row 1 3/4, slip a bead onto the needle,
cable, wave down to row 2, slip a
bead onto the needle, under cable.
Take the needle to the wrong side of
the fabric and work nine cables. Re-
emerge on the front between the
twelfth and thirteenth pleats to the
right of the centre valley. Take the
needle through the pleat on the left.
Repeat the two-step wave cable
combination as before. Continue
working nine cables on the back of the
fabric and two-step wave cable
combination to the end of the row.
Turn the fabric upside down, return to
the centre and complete the row.

Rows 2 - 17. Repeat the previous two
rows fifteen times, adding a bead to
each cable on the right side of the
fabric that doesn't lie alongside a
previously worked cable.

Row 17 - 17 1/2. Repeat row 1 - 1 1/2.

Row 17 1/2 - 18 1/2. Begin at the centre
two pleats on row 17 1/2 with an over
cable. Work wave down to row 17 3/4,
slip a bead onto the needle, cable,
wave down to row 18, slip a bead
onto the needle, cable, wave down to
row 18 1/4, slip a bead onto the needle,
cable, wave down to row 18 1/2, slip a
bead onto the needle, under cable.
Work back up to row 17 1/2 in the
same manner. Continue the sequence
to the end of the row. Turn the fabric
upside down, return to the centre and
complete the row.

Rows 17 3/4 - 19. Repeat the previous
row twice, adding a bead to each over
cable as well as all other cables.

Backsmocking

On the wrong side of the fabric, work
cable along row 18. Only pick up the
tip of each pleat with the needle.

The finished length of the gown from the centre back neckline to the hemline is 85cm (33 ½") for all sizes.

gown front

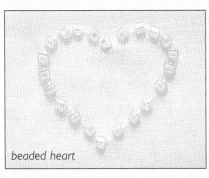

beaded heart

gown sleeve

gown hem

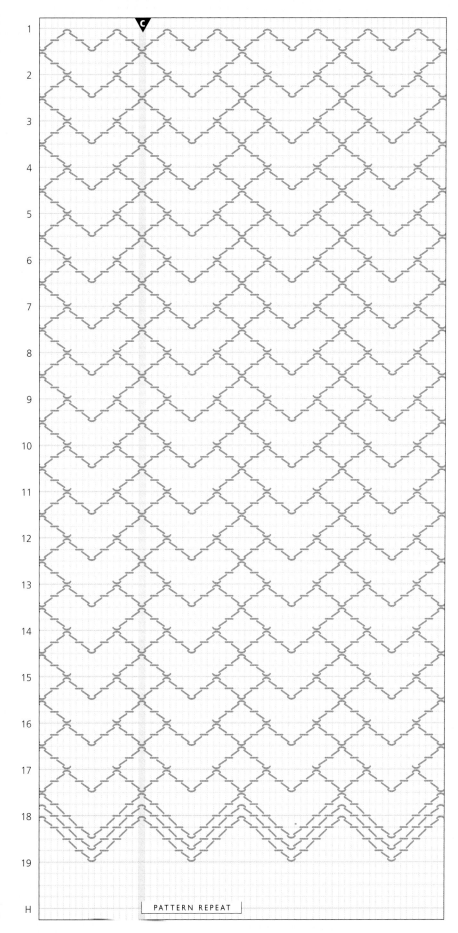

PATTERN REPEAT

PREPARATION FOR EMBROIDERY

See the liftout pattern sheet for the heart template.

Completely assemble the gown following the instructions on pages 128 -131.

Fold the skirt to find the centre front. Using the fabric marker, mark the centre front on each tuck. On the uppermost tuck, measure across 11.5cm (4 1/2") from the centre front and mark. Continue marking the tuck at 11.5cm (4 1/2") intervals around the entire skirt. Repeat on the third tuck.

On the second tuck, measure across 5.75cm (2 1/4") from the centre front and mark. Measure across a further 11.5cm (4 1/2") and mark. Continue marking the tuck at 11.5cm (4 1/2") intervals around the entire skirt. Repeat on the fourth tuck *(diag 2).*

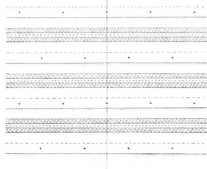

Diag 2

Trace the heart onto a piece of light card and cut out. Centre the heart template on the right side of the first tuck at the centre front. Using the fabric marker, trace around the template. Repeat at each mark around the entire skirt. Transfer hearts to the remaining tucks in the same manner.

EMBROIDERY

Beginning at the centre top of one heart and using running stitch, attach twenty-two beads around the heart outline. Stitch all the remaining marked hearts along the tucks in the same manner.

CONSTRUCTION

See pages 128 - 131.

the Bolero

"I HAVE MANY FLOWERS," HE SAID
"BUT THE CHILDREN ARE THE MOST BEAUTIFUL FLOWERS OF ALL."

OSCAR WILDE (1854 – 1900)

BOLERO ONLY

REQUIREMENTS

Fabric & Lace

Ivory silk organza
40cm x 85cm wide (15 ³/4" x 33 ³/8")
for all sizes

Ivory lace edging
1.5m x 20mm wide (1yd 23" x ³/4")
for all sizes

Ivory lace beading
3.5m x 18mm wide
(3yd 29 ³/4" x ¹¹/16") for all sizes

Ivory lace insertion (floral)
8m x 18mm wide (8yd 27" x ¹¹/16")
for all sizes

Ivory lace insertion (diamonds)
7m x 18mm wide
(7yd 23 ⁵/8" x ¹¹/16") for all sizes

Ivory entredeux beading
3.5m x 11mm wide
(3yd 29 ³/4" x ⁷/16") for all sizes

Narrow ivory entredeux
15cm (6") for all sizes

bolero sleeve

Notions

1 shell heart button 11mm (⁷/16") wide

1 small clear snap fastener

YLI no. 01 antique white silk ribbon
3.5m x 2mm wide (3yd 29 ³/4" x ³/32")

Ivory silk satin ribbon
1m x 6mm wide (1yd 3 ³/8" x ¹/4")

Fine water-soluble fabric marker

PATTERN & CUTTING OUT

See the liftout pattern sheet.

CONSTRUCTION

See pages 131 - 132.

SMOCKING & EMBROIDERY KEY

All smocking and embroidery is worked with one strand of thread unless otherwise specified.

Smocking

Rows 1 - 17 ¹/2 = A
(two-step wave/cable combination), B (beading)

Rows 17 ¹/2 -19 = A
(four-step wave/cable combination), B (beading)

Backsmocking

Row 18 = A (cable)

Embroidery

Hearts = A (running stitch), B (beading)

the Bonnet

REQUIREMENTS

Fabric & Lace

Ivory silk organza
30cm x 70cm wide (11 3/4" x 27 1/2")

Ivory lace edging
1.3m x 20mm wide
(1yd 15 1/4" x 3/4")

Ivory lace beading
30cm x 18mm wide (11 3/4" x 11/16")

Ivory lace insertion (floral)
60cm x 18mm wide (23 1/2" x 11/16")

Narrow ivory entredeux
60cm (23 1/2")

Notions

2 shell heart buttons
11mm (7/16") wide

YLI no. 01 antique white silk ribbon
30cm x 2mm wide (11 3/4" x 3/32")

Ivory silk satin ribbon
50cm x 3mm wide (19 5/8" x 1/8")

Ivory organdie ribbon
1.4m x 38mm wide
(1yd 19" x 1 1/2")

Fine water-soluble fabric marker

PATTERN & CUTTING OUT

See the liftout pattern sheet.

CONSTRUCTION

See page 132.

bonnet detail

gown front

gown back

WHERE CHILDREN ARE,
THERE IS THE GOLDEN AGE.
NOVALIS (1772-1801)

Elegant scrolls, roses and lines of heavenly feather stitch surround the skirt

of this divine white gown. Magnificent lace trims the ruffled brim

of the smocked bonnet and edges the sleeves and hem.

Sizes 3, 6 & 12 months

GOWN & BONNET

REQUIREMENTS

Fabric & Lace

White cotton voile
3.8m x 112cm wide (4yd 5 5/8" x 44")
for all sizes

White cotton lace edging
6.8m x 20mm wide (7yd 15 1/2" x 3/4")

Notions

60cm (23 5/8") white satin mini piping

5 heart-shaped shell buttons
11mm (3/8") wide

White cotton heirloom machine
sewing thread (2 reels)

Fine water-soluble fabric marker

No. 8 crewel needle

No. 10 straw needle

No. 1.6/70 twin sewing machine
needle

Threads

Madeira stranded silk

A = 0815 ultra light shell pink

B = 1910 light beige

C = 2401 cream (5 skeins)

DMC stranded cotton

D = 3032 putty groundings

STITCHES & TECHNIQUES USED

CABLE-WAVE COMBINATION, TWO-STEP TRELLIS, FIVE-STEP TRELLIS, SINGLE FLOWERETTE

BULLION KNOT, DETACHED CHAIN, DOUBLE FEATHER STITCH, FRENCH KNOT, GRANITOS

STEM STITCH, ATTACHING FLAT LACE TO FLAT FABRIC, TWIN NEEDLE PINTUCK

by KRIS RICHARDS

the Gown

Let me look upward into the branches of
The flowering oak and know that it grew great
And strong because it grew slowly and well.

Wilferd A. Peterson

REQUIREMENTS

Fabric & Lace

White cotton voile
3.3m x 112cm wide (3yd 22" x 44")
for all sizes

White cotton lace edging
5.7cm x 20mm wide (6yd 8 1/2" x 3/4")

Notions

60cm (23 5/8") white satin mini piping

5 heart-shaped shell buttons
11mm (3/8") wide

White cotton heirloom machine
sewing thread (2 reels)

Fine water-soluble fabric marker

No. 8 crewel needle

No. 10 straw needle

No. 1.6/70 twin sewing
machine needle

Threads

Madeira stranded silk
A = 0815 ultra light shell pink
B = 1910 light beige
C = 2401 cream (5 skeins)

DMC stranded cotton
D = 3032 putty groundings

PATTERN & CUTTING OUT

*See the liftout pattern sheet for the
pattern and cutting layouts.*

Front overskirt: cut one,
65cm x 112cm wide (25 1/2" x 44")
for all sizes.

Front underskirt: cut one,
79cm x 112cm wide (31" x 44")
for all sizes.

Cut out all other pieces following the
instructions on the liftout pattern sheet.

PREPARATION & PLEATING

Front skirt

Place the two front skirts together,
ensuring the wrong side of the overskirt
is against the right side of the
underskirt. Tack the two layers together
with a row of stitches approximately
5mm (3/16") from the top raw edge.
Work another two rows of tacking,
placing each row approximately 2.5cm
(1") from the previous row *(diag 1)*.

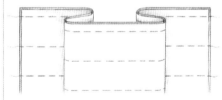

Diag I

Pleat fifteen half space rows (including
two holding rows) with the top
holding row 1cm (3/8") from the top
raw edge. Remove the tacking and
unpick the pleats on both sides for
1cm (3/8"). Tie off the pleating threads
to fit the front blocking guide.

Sleeves

Using pleating threads that are longer
than the width of the fabric, pleat seven
half space rows (including two holding
rows) with the lower holding row
3.5cm (1 3/8") from the lower raw edge.

Flatten out the pleats. Cut two pieces
of lace edging to fit the lower edge
of the sleeves. Attach following the
instructions on page 94.

Unpick the pleating threads for 2.5cm
(1") at each side. Tie off the threads so
the sleeve measures approximately
18cm (7") wide.

SMOCKING

Front skirt

Count the pleats and mark the centre
valley.

Row 1 - 2. Begin on the centre two
pleats on row 2 with an under cable.
Work wave up to row 1. Beginning and
ending with an over cable, work nine
cables. Work wave down to row 2.
Continue working the nine cable-wave
combination to the end of the row.
Turn the fabric upside down, return to
the centre and complete the row.

Row 2 - 3. Repeat the previous row.

Row 4 - 5. Following the graph for
placement, work two-step trellis
between rows 4 and 5.

Row 5 - 7. Following the graph for
placement, work five-step trellis
between rows 5 and 7.

Rows 7 - 13. Work a mirror image of
rows 1 - 7.

Accent stitches

Work single flowerettes at the peak of
each wave on rows 3 and 11. Add a
single flowerette to the centre of each
large diamond on row 7.

Sleeves

Count the pleats and mark the centre valley on each sleeve.

Row 1 - 2. Begin on the centre two pleats on row 1 with an over cable. Work four cables (under, over, under, over), wave down to row 2, under cable, wave up to row 1, nine cables beginning and ending with an over cable. Continue working the cable-wave combination to the end of the row. Turn the fabric upside down, return to the centre and complete the row.

Row 2 - 2³/4. Repeat the previous row, ensuring that the under cable of the wave is slightly above the pleating thread.

Rows 3¹/4 - 5. Work a mirror image of rows 1 - 2³/4.

Accent stitches

Work single flowerettes in the space between the peaks of the waves on row 3.

PREPARATION FOR EMBROIDERY

See the liftout pattern sheet for the embroidery designs.

Front yoke

With the right side of the front yoke uppermost and matching the lower edge of the fabric with the marked line below the design, position the yoke over the embroidery design. Pin in place to prevent movement. Using the fine fabric marker, mark the position of the spray and spots. Rule lines as guides for the double feather stitch.

Skirts

Assemble the gown following the instructions on pages 132 - 135. Open out the button bands on each skirt.

Fold the overskirt in half to find the centre front. Finger press the fold and open out. Beginning at the centre front, place the skirt over the template, aligning the placement line on the template with the lace seam. Using the fabric marker, trace the embroidery motif and mark the ends of the two upper pintucks *(diag 2)*.

Diag 2

Mark the positions for the remaining pintucks and the three lines of double feather stitch. Continue marking the positions of the pintucks and double feather stitch at intervals around the entire skirt. Rule lines to join the marks.

On each side of the central scroll, mark three dots 7mm (⁵/16") apart between the two pintuck lines *(diag 3)*.

Diag 3

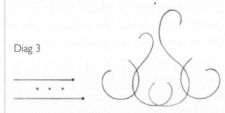

Between the same two lines, mark pairs of dots at evenly spaced intervals approximately 7cm (2 ³/4") apart around the entire skirt.

Fold the underskirt in half to find the centre front. Beginning at the centre front, place the underskirt over the embroidery design. Align the lace seam with the placement line on the template and trace the design using the fabric marker. Repeat around the entire lower skirt. Rule lines for the two rows of double feather stitch.

EMBROIDERY

Front yoke

Beginning from the centre and working towards the armhole each time, stitch the two sections of double feather stitch. Work the bullion rose. Add the detached chains and French knots for the partial daisies and then the detached chain leaves. Embroider the spots last, working a granitos for each one.

Overskirt

Machine stitch the twin needle pintucks and then work the three rows of double feather stitch, ensuring each row is worked in the same direction.

Using stem stitch, embroider the side sections of the scroll and then the middle sections. Work the bullion rose, partial daisies and leaves in the same manner as those on the front yoke. Stitch a granitos spot at each marked dot.

Underskirt

Stitch the two rows of double feather stitch, ensuring they are both worked in the same direction.

Embroider the hearts and scrolls in stem stitch. Begin each motif on the left hand side and work towards the right hand side.

Add a small spray to each scroll motif in the same manner as the spray on the front yoke. Finally, work a granitos spot below each scroll.

CONSTRUCTION

See pages 132 - 135.

In each heart on the underskirt, embroider the name and date for each cherished babe who wears the gown as an historical record of family christenings.

CHILDREN MAY NOT REMEMBER YOU FOR THE MATERIAL THINGS YOU PROVIDED
BUT FOR THE FEELING THAT YOU CHERISHED THEM.
RICHARD L. EVANS

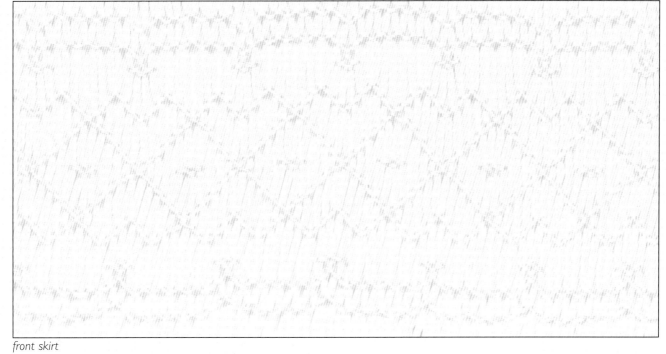

front skirt

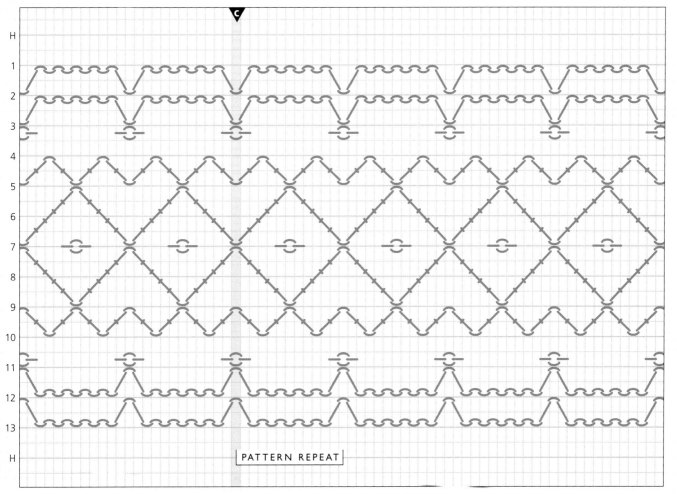

The finished length of the gown from the centre back neckline to the hemline is 85cm (33 ½") for all sizes.

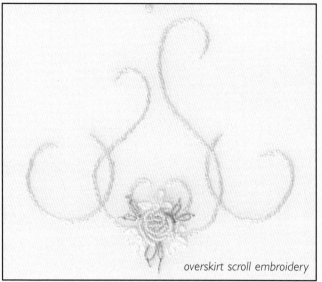

overskirt scroll embroidery

underskirt heart embroidery

overskirt hem detail

underskirt scroll embroidery

RUSSIA

A belt was an extremely important object in peasant Russia. At birth the body of the baby was encircled by a 'belt' often no more elaborate than a single scarlet thread. During the Christening ceremony a child was given its first proper belt and a gift of a cross. Both of these objects became an attribute of the person's life as a Christian. If a child or adult walked about for even a short time without wearing a belt they were not considered a baptized Christian. The belt was to be worn next to the skin at all times. It could not be removed at death since the deceased would wear it at the resurrection of the dead at the Last Judgement.

In the Christian church it is the universal rite of initiation, performed with water in the name of the Trinity (Father, Son and Holy Spirit).

ITALY

The Godparents provide the gown and everything that the baby wears on the day. They also provide something else for the baby to wear after the cake is cut. The Godparents receive a gift from the parents of the baby. Bonboniere given at a Christening will consist of five sugared almonds (either pink or blue) representing health, wealth, love, prosperity and happiness.

ENGLAND

In early English tradition, brides rarely kept their gowns for their daughters. They had the fabric used to make their first child's Christening gown.

The bride often carried a handkerchief that was later sewn into a bonnet for the first baby. Upon the marriage of this child, the bonnet was turned back into a handkerchief for the child to carry on his or her wedding day.

The top tier of the wedding cake was often made as an Irish whiskey cake that was then saved for the Christening of the first baby.

SCOTLAND

On the way to its Christening the child must be carried, at least part of the way, by a young unmarried woman, who must have with her something to eat - usually a piece of bread and cheese. She must present this to the first man that she meets, no matter who or what he may be. The name that a child is to be given must never be spoken aloud until the minister speaks it at the Christening ceremony. If anyone asks they must not be told, nor must the minister be told by word of mouth - he must be handed a piece of paper with the name written on it.

The term Baptism in Greek, 'Baptizein', means 'to dip' or 'to immerse'.

ISLE OF MAN

It was necessary to take great care of children before baptism to protect them from malevolent Fairies who would steal a child and leave a decrepit and emaciated Fairy in its place. One way to protect the child was to place an iron poker on the child when left alone or to tie a red thread around the child's neck. When taking her child to be Christened, a woman would take a piece of bread and cheese with her that she gave to the first person that she met.

Mrs Truman unwound the wrappings of the bundle on her lap, first peeling off the best Paisley shawl in which Charity and her elder cousins had gone to their christenings, then the large white woolly shawl, then the small knitted one, and revealed the baby in long, lacy robes with blue ribbon bows on the shoulders. The impressions this transformation scene should have made was ruined by the smallness of the congregation. Besides the christening party, there were but about a dozen in church, mostly men and boys, and there was none of the rustling and peering and 'pretty dearing' usual on such occasions.

FLORA THOMPSON, STILL GLIDES THE STREAM

the Bonnet

BONNET ONLY (one size)

REQUIREMENTS

Fabric & Lace

White cotton voile

50cm x 112cm wide (19 3/8" x 44")

White cotton lace edging

1.1m x 20mm wide (1yd 7 1/4" x 3/4")

Notions

Fine water-soluble fabric marker

No. 8 crewel needle

No. 10 straw needle

Threads

Madeira stranded silk
A = 0815 ultra light shell pink
B = 1910 light beige
C = 2401 cream

DMC stranded cotton
D = 3032 putty groundings

PATTERN & CUTTING OUT

See the liftout pattern sheet for the pattern and cutting layouts.

Bonnet: cut one, 23cm x 102cm wide (9" x 40").

Cut out all other pieces following the instructions on the liftout pattern sheet.

PREPARATION & PLEATING

Using pleating threads that are longer than the width of the fabric, pleat seven half space rows (including two holding rows) with the lower holding row 2.5cm (1") from the lower raw edge. Unpick the pleating threads for 3cm (1 1/8") at each side.

Flatten out the pleats. Cut a 112cm (44") length of lace edging. Attach the lace to the lower edge following the instructions on page 94. After attaching the lace, rule two lines across the width of the bonnet using the fabric marker. Position one line 1cm (3/8") from the stitchline and the other 5mm (3/16") from the stitchline.

Work double feather stitch between the two marked lines across the entire width of the bonnet before working the smocking.

Fold a 3mm (1/8") double hem at each end and pin. Hand stitch the hem in place.

To form the casing at the back of the bonnet, press under 3mm (1/8") on the remaining long raw edge. Press under a further 1cm (3/8"). Machine stitch in place close to the inner folded edge.

Pull up the pleating threads and tie off to approximately 20cm (8").

SMOCKING

Count the pleats and mark the centre valley.

Row 1 - 2. Begin on the centre two pleats on row 1 with an over cable. Work four cables (under, over, under, over), wave down to row 2, under cable, wave up to row 1, work four cables, (over, under, over, under). Continue working the cable-wave combination to the end of the row. Turn the fabric upside down, return to the centre and complete the row.

Row 2 - 2 3/4. Repeat the previous row, ensuring that the under cable of the wave is slightly above the pleating thread.

Rows 3 1/4 - 5. Work a mirror image of rows 1 - 2 3/4.

Accent stitches

Work single flowerettes in the space between the peaks of the waves on row 3.

EMBROIDERY

After the bonnet is completely assembled, stitch a bullion rose and three pairs of detached chain leaves over the gathering on each tie.

CONSTRUCTION

See page 135.

bonnet

bonnet tie detail

smocking on bonnet

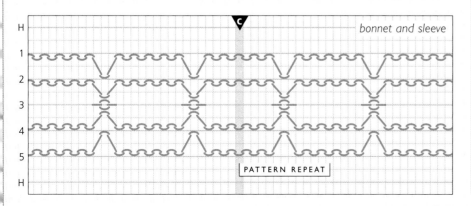

bonnet and sleeve

PATTERN REPEAT

SMOCKING & EMBROIDERY KEY

All smocking is worked with two strands of thread and all embroidery is worked with one strand.

Smocking on front skirt

Rows 1 - 3 and 11 - 13 = C (cable/wave combination)

Rows 4 - 5 and 9 - 10 = C (two-step trellis)

Rows 5 - 9 = C (five-step trellis)

Accent stitches = C (single flowerette)

Smocking on sleeves and bonnet

Rows 1 - 5 = C (cable/wave combination)

Accent stitches = C (single flowerette)

Embroidery

Roses

Centre = B (4 bullion knots, 10 wraps)

Petals = A (4 bullion knots, 15 wraps)

Daisies

Petals = C (detached chain)

Centre = C (French knot, 1 wrap)

Leaves = D (detached chain)

Double feather stitch = C (double feather stitch)

Scrolls = B (stem stitch)

Spots = B (granitos)

Hearts = C (stem stitch)

gown front

gown back

~ HUSH ~

"MY CHILD IS AN ANGEL
GOD GAVE HIM TO ME
I AM NOT WORTHY
THEY TELL ME TO SELL HIM
ANGEL OF HEAVEN
HE IS BEYOND PRICE FOR ME"

PORTUGUESE LULLABY

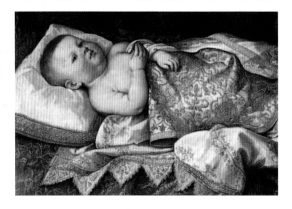

A charming jacket and pants of softest cream wool is smocked with lustrous silk
and trimmed with satin piping and buttons. A matching smocked beret
completes a perfect suit for a tiny gentleman.

Sizes 3, 6 & 12 months

SUIT & BERET

REQUIREMENTS

Fabric

Cream wool challis

Size 3 months: 1.7m x 112cm wide
(1yd 31" x 44")

Size 6 months: 1.8m x 112cm wide
(1yd 35" x 44")

Size 12 months: 1.9m x 112cm wide
(2yd 2 3/4" x 44")

Cream polyester lining

Size 3 months: 1.5m x 112cm wide
(1yd 23" x 44")

Size 6 months: 1.6m x 112cm wide
(1yd 27" x 44")

Size 12 months: 1.7m x 112cm wide
(1yd 31" x 44")

Cream satin
15cm (6") square for all sizes

Notions

4.4m (4yd 29 1/4")
cream satin mini piping

5 self cover buttons 11mm (3/8") wide

1 self cover button 25mm (1") wide

1 small clear snap fastener

White non-roll elastic
50cm x 20mm wide (19 5/8" x 3/4")

Lightweight woven fusible interfacing
30cm x 40cm wide (11 3/4" x 15 3/4")

Fine water-soluble fabric marker

No. 8 crewel needle

Thread

Anchor stranded silk
A = 926 cream

STITCHES & TECHNIQUES USED

VAN DYKE STITCH, TWO-STEP VAN DYKE STITCH, SATIN STITCH BAR

---

by DENISE BAKES

the *Suit*

The finished length of the jacket from the centre back neckline to the hemline is:

Size 3 months: 26.5cm (10 $^3/_8$")
Size 6 months: 30.5cm (12")
Size 12 months: 34.5cm (13 $^5/_8$")

SUIT ONLY

REQUIREMENTS

Fabric

Cream wool challis

Size 3 months: 1.3m x 112cm wide (1yd 15 $^1/_4$" x 44")

Size 6 months: 1.4m x 112cm wide (1yd 19" x 44")

Size 12 months: 1.5m x 112cm wide (1yd 23" x 44")

Cream polyester lining

Size 3 months: 1.2m x 112cm wide (1yd 11 $^1/_4$" x 44")

Size 6 months: 1.3m x 112cm wide (1yd 15 $^1/_4$" x 44")

Size 12 months: 1.4m x 112cm wide (1yd 19" x 44")

Cream satin

15cm (6") square for all sizes

Notions

2.6m (2yd 30 $^3/_8$") cream satin mini piping

5 self cover buttons 11mm ($^3/_8$") wide

1 small clear snap fastener

White non-roll elastic 50cm x 20mm wide (19 $^5/_8$" x $^3/_4$")

Lightweight woven fusible interfacing 30cm x 40cm wide (11 $^3/_4$" x 15 $^3/_4$")

Fine water-soluble fabric marker

No. 8 crewel needle

Thread

Anchor stranded silk
A = 926 cream

PATTERN & CUTTING OUT

See the liftout pattern sheet for the pattern and cutting layouts.

Front: cut two from the wool challis, each

Size 3 months: 26.5cm x 33cm wide (10 $^3/_8$" x 13")

Size 6 months: 30cm x 33cm wide (11 $^3/_4$" x 13")

Size 12 months: 33.5cm x 33cm wide (13 $^1/_8$" x 13").

Cut out all other pieces following the instructions on the liftout pattern sheet.

PREPARATION & PLEATING

On each front, pleat twelve half space rows (including two holding rows) with the top holding row 1cm ($^3/_8$") from the top raw edge. Unpick the pleating threads for 4cm (1 $^1/_2$") on one side of one panel for the armhole shaping and 1cm ($^3/_8$") on the other side for the front opening seam allowance. Repeat on the opposite corners of the remaining panel, ensuring you have a left and a right front *(diag 1)*.

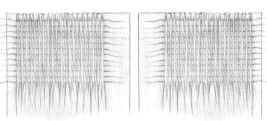

Diag 1

Tie off the pleating threads to fit the front blocking guide.

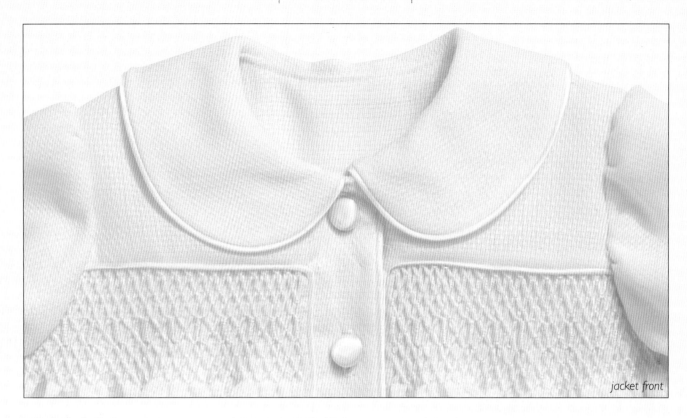

jacket front

SMOCKING

Left front

Row 1. Beginning on the left hand side with an over cable, work cable across the row.

Row 2 - 3. Beginning on row 2, work Van Dyke stitch to the end of the row.

Row 3 - 4. Work a mirror image of the previous row.

Row 4 - 6. Beginning on row 4, work two step Van Dyke to the end of the row.

Rows 6 - 10. Work a mirror image of rows 2 - 6.

Accent stitches

Between rows 5 and 7, work a satin stitch bar over every pair of free pleats.

Righ front

Work the right front as a mirror image of the left front.

CONSTRUCTION

See pages 135 - 139.

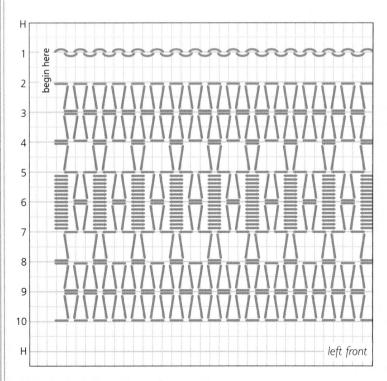

left front

SMOCKING KEY

All smocking is worked with three strands of thread.

Jacket

Row 1 = A (cable stitch)

Rows 2 - 4 = A (Van Dyke stitch)

Rows 4 - 8 = A (two-step Van Dyke stitch)

Rows 8 - 10 = A (Van Dyke stitch)

Accent stitches = A (satin stitch bar)

Beret

Rows 1 - 6 = A (Van Dyke stitch)

"SONS ARE THE ANCHORS OF A MOTHER'S LIFE."
SOPHOCLES, PHAEDRA

the Beret

REQUIREMENTS

Fabric

Cream wool challis
40cm x 112cm wide (15 ³/₄" x 44")

Cream polyester lining
35cm x 112cm wide (13 ³/₄" x 44")

Cream satin
5cm (2") square

Notions

1.8m (1yd 35") cream satin mini piping

1 self cover button 25mm (1") wide

No. 8 crewel needle

Thread

Anchor stranded silk
A = 926 cream

PATTERN & CUTTING OUT

See the liftout pattern sheet for the pattern and cutting layouts.

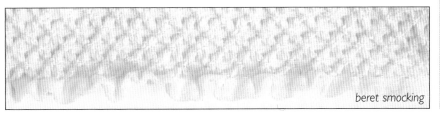

Band: cut one, 9cm x 112cm wide (3 ¹/₂" x 44") from the wool challis.

Cut out all other pieces following the instructions on the liftout pattern sheet.

PREPARATION & PLEATING

With wrong sides together, fold the band in half along the length and press. Tack the two layers together close to the long raw edge.

Pleat seven half space rows (including one holding row at the top) with the last row 5mm (³/₁₆") from the folded edge *(diag 2)*.

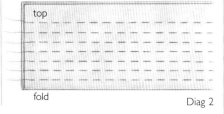

Diag 2

SMOCKING

Row 1 - 2. Begin on the right hand side on row 1. Work Van Dyke stitch to the end of the row.

Row 2 - 3. Work a mirror image of the previous row.

Rows 3 - 5. Repeat rows 1 - 3.

Row 5 - 6. Repeat row 1 - 2.

CONSTRUCTION

See page 139.

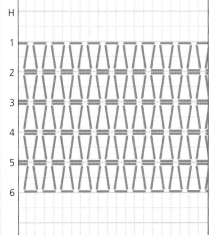

beret smocking

front

Embroidery Stitches

BULLION KNOT

The distance from A to B is the length of the finished knot. To form a straight knot
the number of wraps must cover this distance plus an extra 1 - 2 wraps.

1. Secure the thread on the back of the fabric and bring it to the front at A. Pull the thread through.

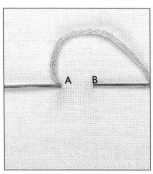

2. Take the needle to the back at B. Re-emerge at A, taking care not to split the thread.

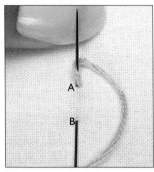

3. Rotate the fabric. Raise the tip of the needle away from the fabric. Wrap the thread clockwise around the needle.

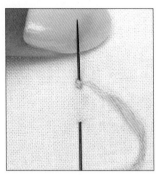

4. Keeping the tip of the needle raised, pull the wrap firmly down onto the fabric.

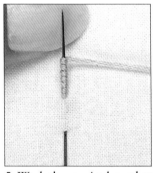

5. Work the required number of wraps around the needle. Pack them down evenly as you wrap.

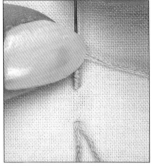

6. Keeping tension on the wraps with your thumb, begin to ease the needle through the fabric and wraps.

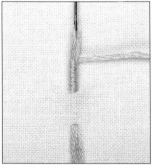

7. Continuing to keep tension on the wraps with your thumb, pull the needle and thread through (thumb not shown).

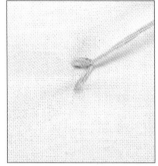

8. Pull the thread all the way through, tugging it away from you to form a small pleat in the fabric. This helps to ensure a tight, even knot.

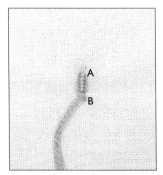

9. Release the thread. Smooth out the fabric and the knot will lie back towards B.

10. To ensure all the wraps are even, gently stroke and manipulate them with the needle while maintaining tension on the thread.

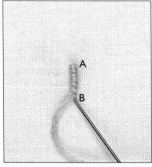

11. Take the needle to the back at B to anchor the knot.

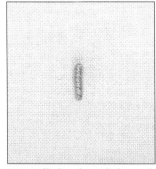

12. Pull the thread through and end off.

BULLION LOOP

This is a variation of the bullion knot. It is formed in the same way as a knot but the distance between A and B is small and the number of wraps is often large.

1. Secure the thread on the back of the fabric and bring it to the front at A. Pull the thread through.

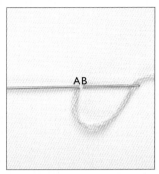

2. Take the needle to the back at B and re-emerge at A, taking care not to split the thread.

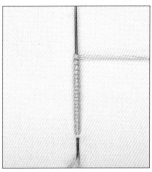

3. Rotate the fabric. Raise the tip of the needle away from the fabric. Wrap the thread around the needle following steps 3 - 5 on page 80.

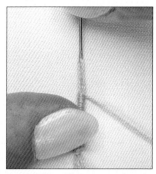

4. Holding the wraps firmly with the left thumb, begin to pull the needle and thread through the wraps.

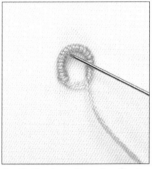

5. Pull the thread all the way through. Using the needle, separate the wraps from the adjacent thread.

6. Hold the wraps in place with your thumb (thumb not shown). Pull the thread towards you to tighten the wraps and curl them into a loop.

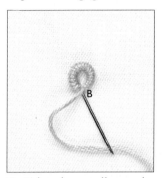

7. Take the needle to the back of the fabric at B.

8. Pull the thread through and end off.

DETACHED CHAIN

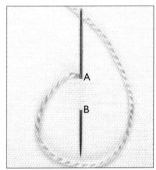

1. Secure the thread on the back of the fabric and bring it to the front at A. Take the needle through the fabric from A to B.

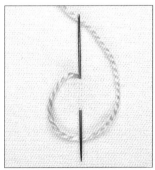

2. Loop the thread under the tip of the needle.

3. Keeping your thumb over the loop, pull the thread through (thumb not shown).

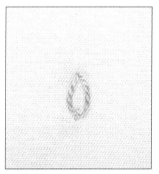

4. Take the thread to the back, just over the loop. Secure the thread on the back of the fabric.

FLY STITCH

Varying the thread tension and the length of the anchoring stitch can alter the look of this stitch.

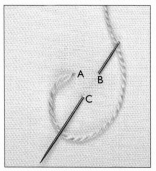

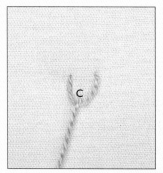

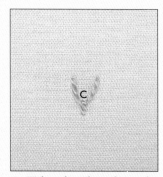

1. Secure the thread on the back of the fabric and bring it to the front at A. This will be the left hand side of the stitch.

2. Take the needle to the back at B and re-emerge at C. Loop the thread under the tip of the needle.

3. Hold the loop in place with your thumb (thumb not shown). Pull the thread until the loop lies snugly against C.

4. Take the thread to the back of the fabric below C to anchor the loop. Secure the thread on the back of the fabric.

FRENCH KNOT

Traditionally, French knots were worked with only one wrap but they can be worked with more.

1. Secure the thread on the back of the fabric and bring it to the front at the position for the knot.

2. Hold the thread firmly approximately 3cm (1 1/8") from the fabric.

3. Take the thread over the needle, ensuring the needle points away from the fabric.

4. Wrap the thread around the needle. Keeping the thread taut, turn the tip of the needle towards the fabric.

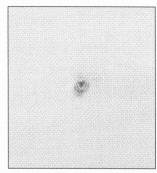

5. Take the tip of the needle to the back of the fabric approximately 1 - 2 fabric threads away from where it emerged.

6. Slide the knot down the needle onto the fabric. Pull the thread until the knot is firmly around the needle.

7. Push the needle through the fabric. Hold the knot in place with your thumb and pull the thread through.

8. Pull until the loop of thread completely disappears. Secure the thread on the back of the fabric.

COLONIAL KNOT

A colonial knot is similar in appearance to a French knot but is slightly larger and firmer.
Also known as a candlewicking knot, it can be worked alone or to fill a shape.

1. Secure the thread on the back of the fabric and bring it to the front at the position for the knot.

2. Hold the thread loosely in your left hand. With your right hand, place the tip of the needle over the thread.

3. Hook the needle under the thread where it emerges from the fabric.

4. With your left hand, take the thread over the tip of the needle to form a loop. Shorten the loop.

5. Take the thread under the tip of the needle to form a figure eight around the needle.

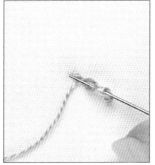

6. Take the tip of the needle to the back of the fabric approximately two fabric threads away from where the thread first emerged.

7. Pull the wraps firmly against the fabric.

8. Keeping the thread taut, push the needle through the knot to the back of the fabric.

9. Hold the knot and loop on the fabric with your thumb and continue to pull the thread through (thumb not shown).

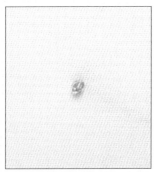

10. Pull until the loop disappears. Secure the thread on the back of the fabric.

CHILDREN BORN
OF FAIRY STOCK
NEVER NEED FOR
SHIRT OR FROCK,
NEVER WANT FOR
FOOD OR FIRE,
ALWAYS GET THEIR
HEART'S DESIRE.

ROBERT GRAVES,
I'D LOVE TO BE
A FAIRY'S CHILD

STEM STITCH

The thread must always be kept below the needle when working stem stitch.

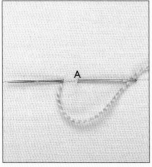 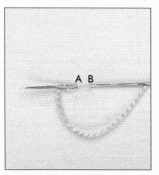  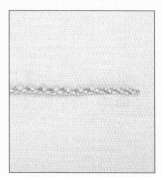

1. Mark a line on the fabric. Bring the thread to the front at the left hand end of the line. With the thread below the needle, take the needle to the back at A and re-emerge at the end of the line.

2. Pull the thread through. Again with the thread below the needle, take the needle to the back at B and re-emerge at A.

3. Pull the thread through. Continue working stitches in the same manner, always keeping the thread below the needle.

4. To end off, take the needle to the back for the last stitch and do not re-emerge. Secure the thread.

BLANKET STITCH

Blanket stitch was traditionally used to edge blankets and it can be used as both an edging stitch and a surface embroidery stitch.

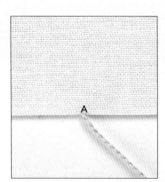 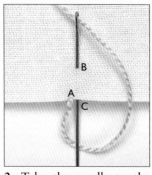  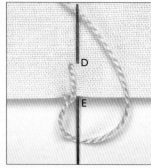

1. Secure the thread on the back of the fabric and bring it to the front at A.

2. Take the needle to the back at B and re-emerge at C. Ensure the thread is under the tip of the needle.

3. Pull the thread through until the stitch sits snugly against the edge of the fabric but does not distort it.

4. Take the needle to the back at D and re-emerge at E. Again, ensure the thread is under the tip of the needle.

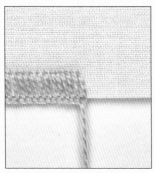  

5. Pull the thread through. Continue working stitches in the same manner.

6. Take the thread to the back of the fabric just over the last loop and end off.

BUTTONHOLE STITCH

Buttonhole stitch creates a row of knots or 'purls' along the cut edge. These reinforce the edge.

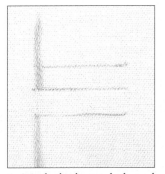

1. Mark the buttonhole and cut the opening. Take the needle through the opening and emerge on the lower line. Pull through leaving a 2cm (³/₄") tail.

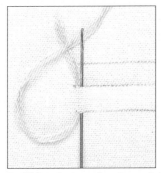

2. Take the needle through the opening and re-emerge next to the first stitch.

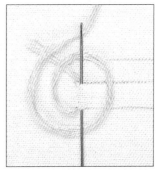

3. Wrap the thread clockwise behind the eye and then the tip of the needle.

4. Pull the thread towards you and then upwards and away from you until the loop slips along the stitch towards the opening. A 'purl' forms at the cut edge.

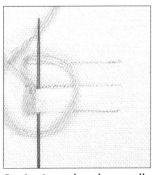

5. Again, take the needle through the opening and re-emerge next to the previous stitch. Wrap the thread clockwise as before.

6. Pull the thread through until the 'purl' forms at the cut edge. Keeping the stitches close together, continue in the same manner to the end of the opening.

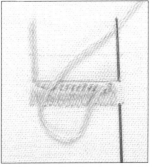

7. To work the bar tack, take the needle through the opening and re-emerge next to the previous stitch. Do not wrap the thread around the needle.

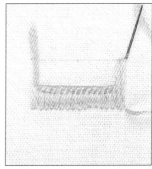

8. Pull the thread through. Work 3 - 4 straight stitches across the end between the upper and lower marked lines.

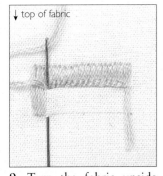

9. Turn the fabric upside down. Bring the thread to the front through the opening. Take the needle back through the opening and re-emerge on the lower line.

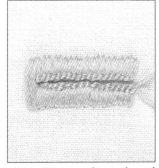

10. Wrap the thread clockwise around the needle as before and pull the thread through. Continue working stitches to the end of the opening.

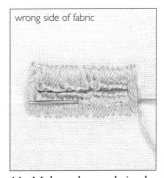

11. Make a bar tack in the same manner as before, finishing with the thread on the back of the fabric. Turn the fabric over to the back. Slide the needle behind the stitches without going through the fabric.

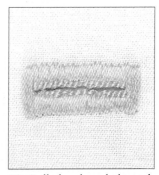

12. Pull the thread through and trim. Secure the beginning tail in the same manner.

DOUBLE BACK STITCH - SHADOW WORK

When beginning, position the waste knot at least 7.5cm (3") from the first stitch.
To work a curve, the stitches on the inside are made smaller than those on the outside of the curve.

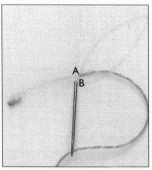

1. Begin with a waste knot. Bring the needle to the front at A, on the upper side. Pull the thread through and take the needle to the back at B.

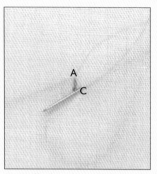

2. Pull the thread through. Re-emerge at C on the lower side, directly opposite A.

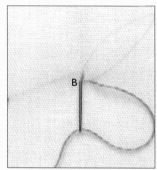

3. Pull the thread through. Take the needle to the back at B, using the same hole in the fabric as before.

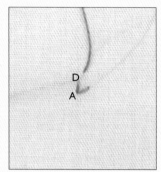

4. Pull the thread through. Re-emerge at D on the upper side and just beyond A.

5. Pull the thread through. Take the needle to the back at A, using exactly the same hole in the fabric as before.

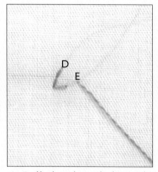

6. Pull the thread through. Re-emerge at E on the lower side, directly opposite D. Pull the thread through.

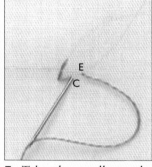

7. Take the needle to the back at C, using exactly the same hole in the fabric as before.

8. Continue in the same manner until reaching the crossover point. The last stitch on both sides emerges at this point.

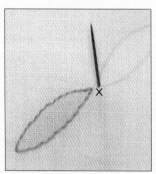

9. Bring the thread to the front on the lower side, just beyond the crossover point (X).

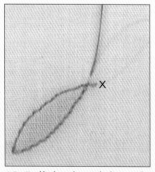

10. Pull the thread through. Take the thread to the back at the crossover point, using exactly the same hole in the fabric as before. Re-emerge on the upper side directly opposite X.

DOUBLE BACK STITCH - SHADOW WORK CONTINUED

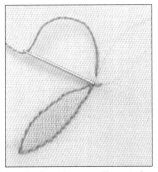

11. Take the needle to the back of the fabric at the crossover point as before.

wrong side of fabric

12. Pull the thread through and continue stitching in the same manner. Secure thread on back of fabric behind the back stitches.

13. Shadow work on the right side of the fabric.

GRANITOS

Granitos are quick and easy to stitch and are formed by working straight stitches through exactly the same holes in the fabric.

TELL ME, PRAISE,
AND TELL ME, LOVE,
WHAT ARE YOU BOTH
THINKING OF?
'O, WE THINK,' SAID
LOVE, SAID PRAISE,
'NOW OF CHILDREN
AND THEIR WAYS.'

WILLIAM BRIGHTY RANDS,
PRAISE AND LOVE

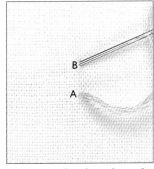

1. Secure the thread on the back of the fabric and bring it to the front at A. Pull the thread through and take it to the back at B.

2. Pull the thread through. Re-emerge at A, taking care to come through exactly the same hole in the fabric as before.

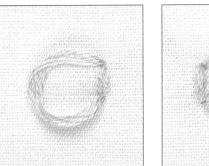

3. Pull the thread through. Take the needle to the back at B through exactly the same hole in the fabric as before.

4. Loop the thread to the left of the first stitch and begin to gently pull the thread through.

5. Pull until the stitch lies alongside the first stitch. Work a third stitch, looping the thread to the right of the first stitch.

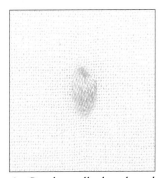

6. Gently pull the thread through. Work the required number of stitches in the same manner, always alternating from side to side. Secure the thread on the back of the fabric.

DOUBLE FEATHER STITCH

Ruling three parallel lines on the fabric as a guide for your stitching will help you keep the stitches straight and even.

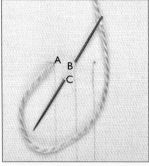

1. Secure the thread on the back of the fabric and bring it to the front at A. Insert the needle at B, directly opposite A. Re-emerge at C, halfway between and slightly lower than A and B.

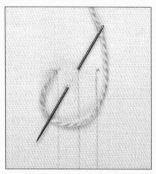

2. Loop the thread to the right and under the needle.

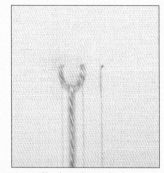

3. Pull the thread through in a downward movement. Hold the thread firmly with your thumb (thumb not shown).

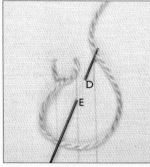

4. Keeping the thread taut, loop it to the right. Take the needle from D to E, ensuring the loop is under the tip of the needle.

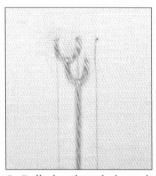

5. Pull the thread through in a downward movement and hold it firmly with your thumb (thumb not shown).

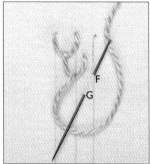

6. Keeping the thread taut, loop it to the right again. Take the needle from F to G. Ensure the loop is under the tip of the needle.

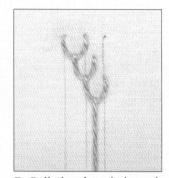

7. Pull the thread through as before.

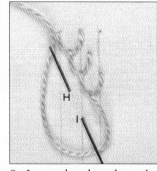

8. Loop the thread to the left and hold in place firmly with your thumb. Take the needle from H to I, ensuring the loop is under the tip of the needle.

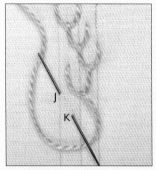

9. Pull the thread through as before. Again, loop the thread to the left and firmly hold in place. Take the needle from J to K.

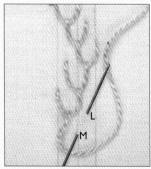

10. Pull the thread through as before. Loop the thread to the right and firmly hold in place. Take the needle from L to M.

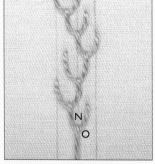

11. Pull the thread through as before. Again, loop the thread to the right and firmly hold in place. Take the needle from N to O and pull the thread through.

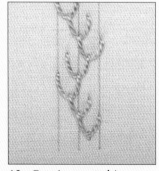

12. Continue working two stitches to the left and two to the right. To end off, take the needle to the back just over the last loop. Pull the thread through and end off.

RUNNING STITCH

Running stitch is quick and easy to work. It looks more effective when the stitches on the right side of the fabric are longer than the stitches on the wrong side.

1. Mark a line on the fabric. Secure the thread on the back of the fabric and bring it to the front at the right hand end of the line.

2. Take a small stitch, skimming the needle beneath the fabric along the line.

3. Pull the thread through. Take another stitch in the same manner as before, ensuring the stitch is the same length as the previous stitch.

4. Continue in the same manner to the end. Take the thread to the back of the fabric and end off.

STRAIGHT STITCH

Straight stitch is the simplest of stitches and forms the basis of many complex stitches.

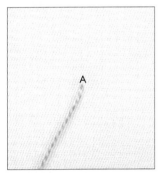 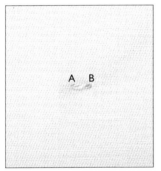  

1. Secure the thread on the back of the fabric and bring it to the front at A.

2. Take the needle to the back at B. Pull the thread through.

3. Work subsequent stitches in the same manner. Secure the thread on the back of the fabric.

4. Several straight stitches worked together.

THREADS

WHEN USING MULTIPLE STRANDS OF STRANDED THREAD, ALWAYS SEPARATE THEM AND THEN PUT THEM BACK TOGETHER. THIS IS KNOWN AS 'STRIPPING' THE THREAD AND ALLOWS YOUR STITCHES TO BETTER COVER THE FABRIC.

USE LENGTHS OF COTTON THREAD APPROXIMATELY 50CM (20") LONG. WHEN WORKING WITH RAYON THREAD, USE SHORTER LENGTHS AS THIS WILL MINIMISE TWISTING AND TANGLING.

IF YOUR THREAD BECOMES TOO TWISTED OR UNTWISTED, LET THE NEEDLE DANGLE. THE THREAD WILL SPIN BACK TO THE CORRECT AMOUNT OF TWIST.

EYELET

An eyelet is made by creating a small hole and then securing the edge
with smooth, regular overcasting stitches.

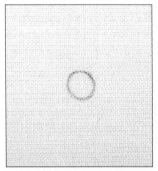

1. Mark the position for the eyelet with a small circle.

2. Using a dressmaker's awl, pierce the centre of the circle from the right side of the fabric.

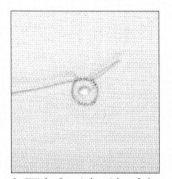

3. With the right side of the fabric facing you, work a small running stitch on the marked line. Pull the thread through, leaving a tail of approximately 3mm (1/8"").

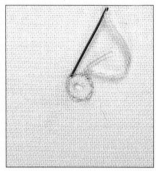

4. Work small running stitches around the circle. On the last stitch, take the needle through the first stitch, splitting it.

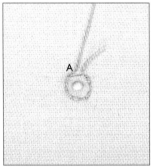

5. Pull the thread through. Re-pierce the hole with the awl. Bring the thread to the front of the fabric just outside the running stitch (A).

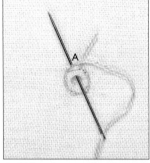

6. Take the needle through the hole at the centre and re-emerge next to A.

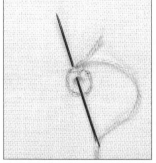

7. Pull the thread through. Take the needle through the centre hole again and re-emerge alongside the previous stitch.

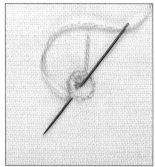

8. Continue working overcasting stitches closely together. Keep turning the fabric to maintain a consistent fanning of the stitches.

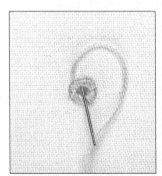

9. Trim the tail close to the fabric. When reaching the start-ing position, take the needle to the back of the fabric through the hole.

10. To end off, take the thread under the overcast stitches on the back of the fabric and secure.

11. Using the awl, carefully re-pierce the hole from the back of the fabric.

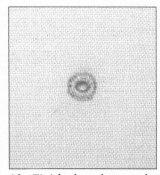

12. Finished eyelet on the right side of the fabric.

RUSSIAN CHAIN STITCH VARIATION

This interesting variation of chain stitch creates a pretty, braided effect
and is ideal for adding decorative lines to garments.

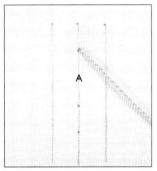

1. Rule three lines on the fabric 5mm ($^3/_{16}$") apart and mark the centre line at 5mm ($^3/_{16}$") intervals. Secure the thread on the back and bring it to the front on the first mark below the top of the centre line (A).

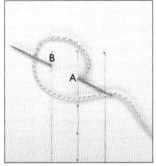

2. Take the needle from A to B, on the left hand line and approximately 3mm ($^1/_8$") above A. Loop the thread behind the tip of the needle.

3. Pull the thread through. Take the needle to the back of the fabric just over the loop.

4. Pull the thread through. Re-emerge at A on the centre line.

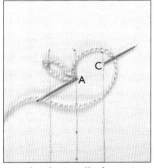

5. Take the needle from A to C, on the right hand line and approximately 3mm ($^1/_8$") above A. Loop the thread behind the tip of the needle.

6. Pull the thread through. Take the needle to the back of the fabric just over the loop.

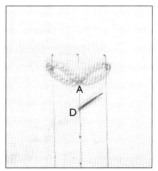

7. Pull the thread through. Re-emerge at D, the mark below A on the centre line.

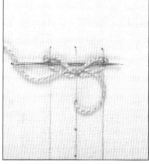

8. Pull the thread through. Take the needle, eye first, behind the top thread of each chain stitch above.

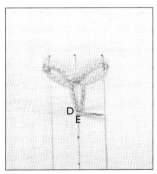

9. Pull the thread through. Take the needle to the back of the fabric at D and re-emerge directly below at E.

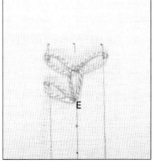

10. Pull the thread through. Take the needle to the back at E and work a chain stitch to the left.

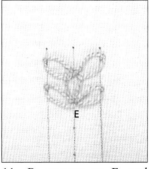

11. Re-emerge at E and work a chain stitch to the right.

12. Continue working the sequence of three chain stitches to the end of the line. Take the thread to the back of the fabric and end off.

GATHERED RIBBON FLOWER

Varying the number of evenly spaced sections the length of ribbon is divided into,
will alter the number of petals created.

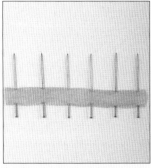

1. Cut a piece of ribbon the required length. Leaving approximately 1cm (³/₈") at each end, mark the ribbon into five evenly spaced sections.

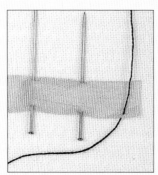

2. Using a length of fine sewing thread, bring it to the front on the edge of the ribbon at the first mark. Leave a tail of thread approximately 5cm (2").

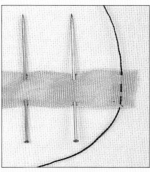

3. Work small running stitches across the ribbon to the opposite edge.

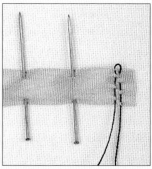

4. Take the thread over the edge. Work running stitches almost back to the opposite edge.

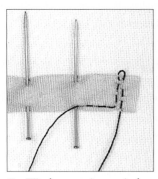

5. Work running stitches close to the edge until reaching the second mark.

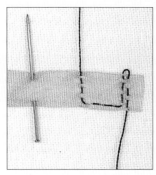

6. Turn and stitch to the opposite edge of the ribbon.

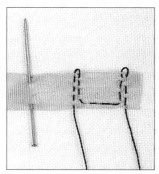

7. Again, take the thread over the edge and work running stitches almost back to the opposite edge.

8. Continue working running stitches in this manner until reaching the last mark.

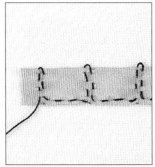

9. Stitch across to the opposite edge and back again in the same manner as before.

10. Pull up the running stitches to gather the ribbon and form the petals.

11. Push the tails of ribbon to the back and tie the two ends of thread together. Trim any excess ribbon.

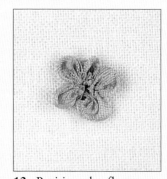

12. Position the flower on the fabric and secure with tiny stab stitches around the centre. End off the thread on the back of the fabric.

Heirloom Sewing

ATTACHING FLAT LACE TO FLAT LACE

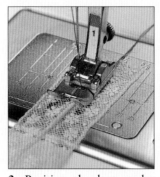

1. With the right sides uppermost, place two pieces of lace side by side. Position the lace so the headings just overlap and the pattern matches.

2. Position the lace under the presser foot so that the overlapped headings are aligned with the centre of the foot and approximately 1cm (³/₈") of lace extends behind the foot.

3. Use a short zigzag stitch that just clears each side of the headings. As you begin to stitch, hold the tails of thread taut behind the pressure foot to engage the tension.

4. Complete the stitching and press.

ATTACHING FLAT LACE TO FLAT FABRIC

The most commonly used heirloom sewing technique is known as 'rolling and whipping'.
It creates a firm, but fine seam.
The stitch length of the zigzag should be short, although not as short as satin stitch.

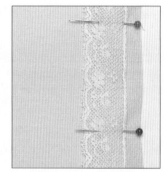

1. With right sides together, place the lace on the fabric. Position the lace heading on the stitchline and pin in place.

2. Stitch along the centre of the lace heading using a short straight stitch.

3. Trim the raw edge of the fabric to within 3mm (¹/₈") of the lace heading.

4. Using a zigzag stitch wide enough to cover the lace heading and clear the fabric on the right hand side, begin to stitch.

5. Continue working zigzag stitch to the end. The seam allowance will roll into the stitching.

6. Press the seam towards the fabric and the lace away from the fabric.

ATTACHING FLAT LACE TO ENTREDEUX

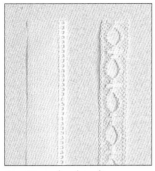

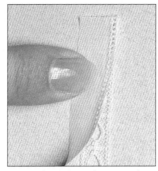

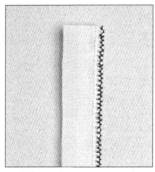

1. Trim the heading away from one side of the entredeux, taking care not to cut the stitching.

2. With right sides together, place the trimmed edge of the entredeux over the edge of the lace heading. Pin in place.

3. Adjust the zigzag stitch so the needle goes into each hole of the entredeux and swings wide enough to just clear the lace heading. Stitch.

4. Press the lace and entredeux open.

ATTACHING FLAT FABRIC TO ENTREDEUX

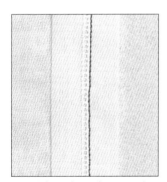

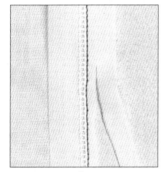

1. With right sides together and raw edges even, place the untrimmed heading of the entredeux onto the fabric. Using a short stitch length, 'stitch in the ditch' of the entredeux.

2. Trim the seam to approximately 3mm (¹/₈") as evenly as possible to ensure a straight seam. Ensure there are no 'whiskers' on the trimmed edge.

3. Stitch, using a zigzag stitch slightly longer than satin stitch. The stitch width should align with the previous stitchline on the left hand side and just clear the fabric on the right hand side.

4. Press the seam towards the fabric and the entredeux away from the fabric.

HEIRLOOM SEWING

ALWAYS CHECK ENTREDEUX CAREFULLY TO ENSURE THAT THE RIGHT SIDE WILL BE ON THE OUTSIDE OF YOUR GARMENT. THE STITCHING ON THE RIGHT SIDE WILL APPEAR SMOOTHER.

STARCHING LACES, ENTREDEUX AND FABRIC WILL MAKE THEM EASIER TO HANDLE. USE SEVERAL LIGHT APPLICATIONS OF SPRAY STARCH, PRESSING BETWEEN EACH ONE, RATHER THAN ONE HEAVY APPLICATION.

USE FINE HEIRLOOM MACHINE SEWING THREAD AND PRESS EACH ROW OF STITCHING BEFORE WORKING THE NEXT.

ATTACHING GATHERED LACE TO FLAT LACE

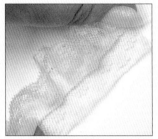

1. Pull the top thread in the lace heading to gather one piece of lace. With the right sides uppermost and the gathered lace on the left hand side, place two pieces of lace side by side. Position the lace so the headings just overlap.

2. Position the lace under the presser foot so that the overlapped headings are aligned with the centre of the foot and approximately 1cm (³⁄₈") of lace extends behind the foot.

3. Use a short zigzag stitch that just clears each side of the headings. As you begin to stitch, hold the tails of thread taut behind the presser foot to engage the tension.

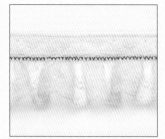

4. Complete the stitching and press.

ATTACHING GATHERED LACE TO ENTREDEUX

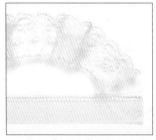

1. Starch and press the entredeux and cut away the heading from one side. Gather the lace by pulling the top thread in the lace heading.

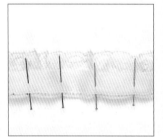

2. Pin the lace and entredeux right sides together with the trimmed edge of the entredeux even with the top edge of the lace.

3. Stitch with the entredeux uppermost and using a zigzag stitch. Adjust the settings so the needle will go into each hole on the left hand side and just clear the edge on the right hand side.

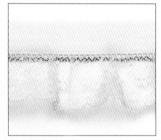

4. Press the seam and entredeux flat, taking care not to press the lace.

ATTACHING GATHERED FABRIC TO ENTREDEUX

1. With right sides together, raw edges even and the wrong side of the entredeux uppermost, pin the untrimmed entredeux to the gathered fabric. Using a straight stitch 'stitch in the ditch'.

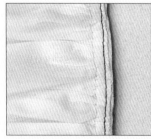

2. Trim the seam, ensuring the fabric seam allowance is slightly narrower than the entredeux seam.

3. Stitch with the fabric uppermost and a zigzag stitch slightly longer than satin stitch. The stitching should align with the previous stitchline on the left hand side and just clear the raw edge of the entredeux on the right hand side.

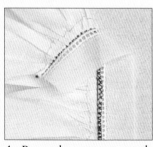

4. Press the seam towards the fabric and the entredeux away from the fabric.

ATTACHING LACE BEADING & EDGING TO NET

This method is used in *Gossamer* and results in a perfectly neat finish to the seam.

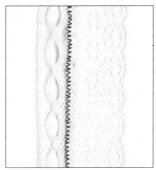
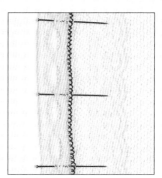

1. Join the lace beading to the lace edging following the step-by-step instructions for attaching flat lace to flat lace.

2. Place the lace onto the net with wrong sides together. Align the remaining heading of the beading with the edge of the netting and pin.

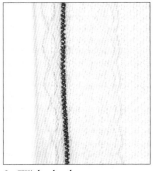
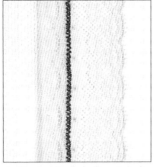

3. With the lace uppermost and using a zigzag stitch, stitch along the previous line of stitching.

4. Press the beading to the right side of the net.

5. Using a zigzag stitch just wider than the lace heading, stitch along the lace heading.

6. Press. Thread ribbon through the beading.

MACHINE PIN STITCH

Also known as hemstitch and point de Paris stitch, this lovely stitch can be worked either by hand or machine. It can be used to create the look of fine entredeux.

1. Use several light applications of spray starch, pressing between each one, until the fabric and lace are crisp.

2. With the wrong side of the lace to the right side of the fabric, position the lace heading on the fabric stitchline. Stitch the lace to the fabric using a narrow zigzag stitch no wider than the lace heading.

3. Cut the excess fabric from behind the lace, trimming close to the zigzag stitching.

4. Using a suitable hemstitch or wing needle, stitch so the pin stitch holes lie beside the lace heading in the fabric and the sideways stitches enclose the lace heading. Press.

INSERTING LACE

Use a fabric marker or lead pencil to mark guidelines on the fabric before positioning the lace insertion.

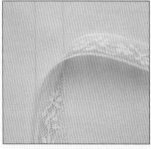

1. With the right side facing up, lay a length of lace insertion on the right side of the fabric between the marked guidelines.

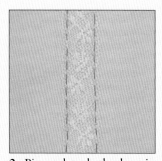

2. Pin and tack the lace in place, stitching just inside the lace heading.

3. Using a small machine straight stitch, stitch along both edges of the lace. Remove the tacking.

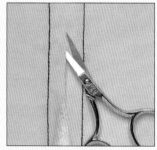

4. Separate the layers and carefully cut along the centre of the fabric behind the lace.

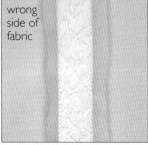

5. On the wrong side of the fabric, press the seam allowance away from the lace.

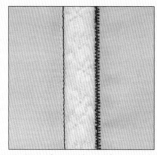

6. On the right side, work zigzag stitch over the previous lines of stitching.

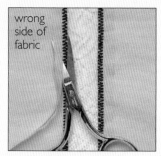

7. On the wrong side, trim the seam allowance close to the zigzag stitching.

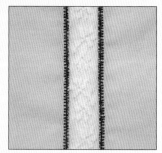

8. Remove any visible guidelines and press.

TWIN NEEDLE PINTUCKS

Rule a line to mark the position of the first tuck. This tuck will then become a guide for the placement of subsequent tucks. A size 1.6/70 twin needle is the most commonly used twin needle in heirloom sewing.

1. Position the fabric so the marked line is centred under the centre groove of the pintuck foot. Lower the needle into the fabric. As you begin stitching, hold the tails of thread to engage the tension.

2. Using a short straight stitch, stitch along the entire line to complete the first pintuck.

3. Position the first pintuck in a groove on one side of the presser foot. Keeping the first pintuck within this groove, stitch a second pintuck. This ensures the pintucks are parallel.

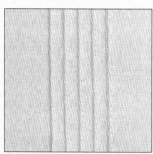

4. Continue working pintucks in the same manner at the required spacing.

Smocking Stitches

CABLE STITCH

When working cable stitch, always keep the needle horizontal and in the same position on the pleating row. The needle position does not change at all, only the thread position.

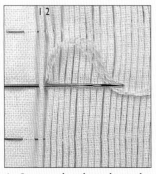

1. Secure the thread on the back of the fabric. Bring it to the front between pleats 1 and 2. Take the needle from right to left through the first pleat.

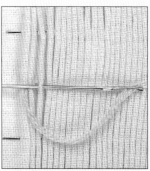

2. Pull the thread through. With the thread below, take the needle through the next pleat. This will form an under cable.

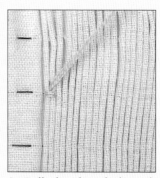

3. Pull the thread through until the stitch is snug against the pleats. Gently tug downwards to reposition the thread for the next stitch.

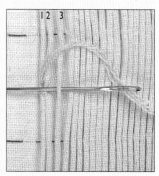

4. With the thread above the needle, take the needle through pleat 3. This will form an over cable.

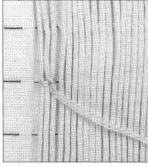

5. Pull the thread through as before. Gently tug upwards to position the thread for the next stitch.

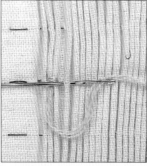

6. With the thread below the needle, take the needle through the next pleat for the second under cable.

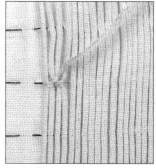

7. Pull the thread through and tug as in step 3.

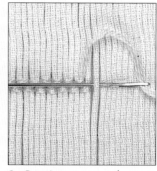

8. Continue across the row, alternating the thread position and keeping the needle horizontal and aligned with the pleating row for each stitch.

"HUSH BABY.
I WILL KEEP YOU
SAFE."
PAM BROWN

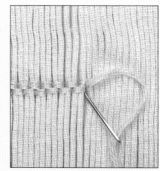

9. After completing the last stitch, take the needle to the back of the fabric through the valley in the middle of the last stitch.

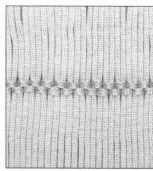

10. Pull the thread through and end off.

WAVE STITCH

Wave stitch is one of the most commonly used smocking stitches and combines well
with other stitches to create a variety of designs.

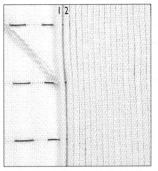

1. Secure the thread on the back. Bring it to the front between pleats 1 and 2. Take the needle from right to left through pleat 1 and pull through.

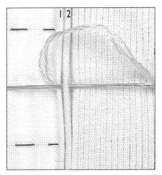

2. With the thread above the needle, take the needle from right to left through pleat 2.

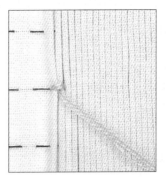

3. Pull the thread through forming an over cable.

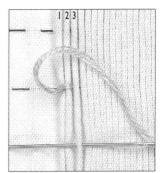

4. Keeping the thread above and the needle horizontal, take the needle from right to left through pleat 3 on the pleating row below.

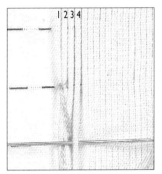

5. Pull the thread through. With the thread below the needle, take the needle from right to left through pleat 4.

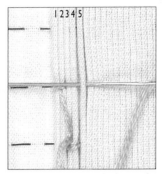

6. Pull the thread through. Keeping the thread below, take the needle from right to left through pleat 5 on the upper pleating row.

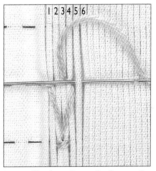

7. Pull the thread through. With the thread above the needle, take the needle from right to left through pleat 6.

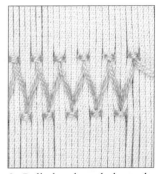

8. Pull the thread through. Continue across the row in the same manner, ending with a cable stitch.

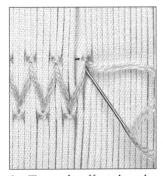

9. To end off, take the needle to the back of the fabric through the valley of the last stitch.

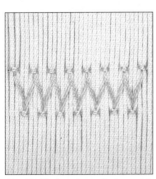

10. Pull the thread through and end off.

"...THE DAUGHTER IS
FOR THE MOTHER
AT ONCE
HER DOUBLE AND
ANOTHER PERSON."

SIMONE DE BEAUVOIR
THE SECOND SEX

CABLE-WAVE COMBINATION

Any number of cable stitches can be used between the wave stitches
as long as it is an odd number of stitches.

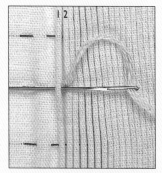

1. Secure the thread on the back of the fabric. Bring the thread to the front in the valley between pleats 1 and 2. Take the needle from right to left through pleat 1.

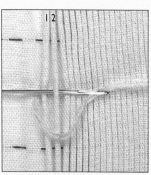

2. Pull the thread through. With the thread below the needle, take the needle from right to left through pleat 2.

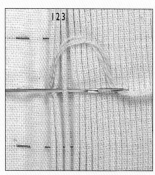

3. Pull the thread through to form an under cable. With the thread above the needle, take the needle from right to left through pleat 3.

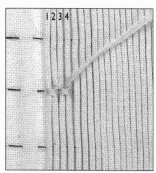

4. Pull the thread through to form an over cable. Work an under cable.

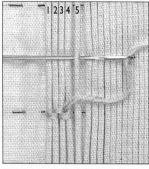

5. Keeping the thread below and the needle horizontal, take the needle from right to left through pleat 5 on the pleating row above.

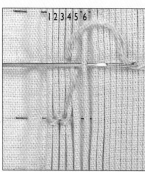

6. Pull the thread through. With the thread above the needle, take the needle from right to left through pleat 6.

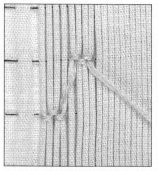

7. Pull the thread through. Work two more cable stitches (under, over).

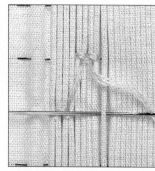

8. Keeping the thread above and the needle horizontal, take the needle from right to left through the next pleat on the pleating row below.

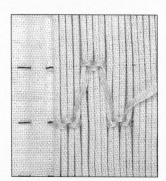

9. Pull the thread through. Work three cables (under, over, under).

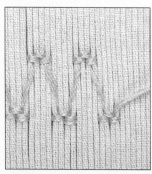

10. Continue across the row, ending with a cable stitch.

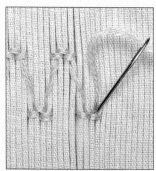

11. After completing the last stitch, take the needle to the back of the fabric through the valley in the middle of the last stitch.

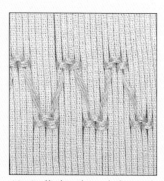

12. Pull the thread through and end off.

SINGLE FLOWERETTE

Whether worked as single or double flowerettes, these dainty accent stitches always cover four pleats.
Pick up approximately two thirds of each pleat and work with a loose tension.

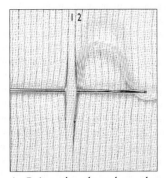

1. Bring the thread to the front in the valley between the first and second pleats. Take the needle from right to left through the first pleat.

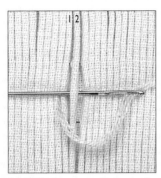

2. Pull the thread through. With the thread below the needle, take the needle from right to left through the second pleat.

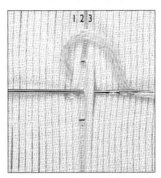

3. Pull the thread through to form an under cable. With the thread above the needle, take the needle from right to left through the third pleat.

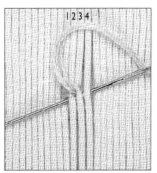

4. Pull the thread through. With the thread above the needle, take the needle from right to left through pleats 4, 3 and 2. Emerge just below the first stitch.

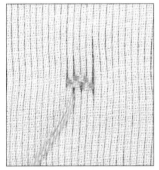

5. Pull the thread through to form an under cable.

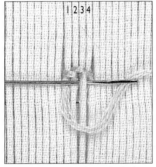

6. With the thread below the needle, take the needle from right to left through the third pleat.

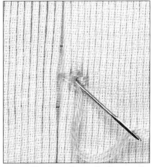

7. Pull the thread through. Take the needle to the back of the fabric through the centre of the stitches.

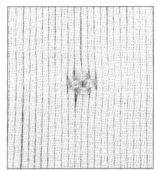

8. Pull the thread through and end off.

READING DESIGN GRAPHS

EACH VERTICAL LINE REPRESENTS A PLEAT AND THE SPACES BETWEEN THE LINES REPRESENT THE VALLEYS. BOLD HORIZONTAL LINES INDICATE THE PLEATING ROWS. BETWEEN THESE LINES, NARROWER LINES ARE OFTEN USED TO INDICATE THE QUARTER AND HALF SPACES BETWEEN THE PLEATING ROWS. • TAKE NOTE OF THE CENTRE OF THE DESIGN AS SHOWN ON THE GRAPH AND ENSURE THE CENTRE OF YOUR SMOCKING IS THE SAME. • MOST GRAPHS DO NOT SHOW THE ENTIRE SMOCKING DESIGN BUT DO INDICATE PATTERN REPEATS. THESE ARE YOUR GUIDE FOR COMPLETING THE DESIGN ACROSS THE ENTIRE WIDTH OF YOUR SMOCKED PIECE. • WHEN WORKING TRELLIS STITCH, COUNT THE DIAGONAL SECTIONS BETWEEN THE SLASHES, NOT THE SLASHES, TO DETERMINE THE NUMBER OF STITCHES REQUIRED. THE SLASHES SHOW WHERE THE NEEDLE GOES THROUGH THE PLEATS AS YOU TRAVEL UP AND DOWN.

STEPPED WAVE-CABLE COMBINATION

Always keep the thread above the needle when working downwards
and below the needle when working upwards.

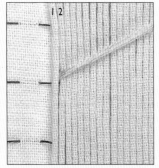

1. Secure the thread on the back of the fabric and bring it to the front between pleats 1 and 2.

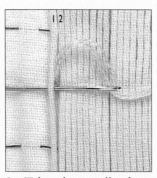

2. Take the needle from right to left through pleat 1 ready to begin stitching.

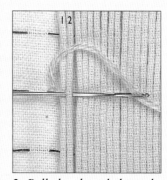

3. Pull the thread through. With the thread above the needle, take the needle from right to left through pleat 2.

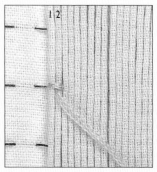

4. Pull the thread through forming an over cable.

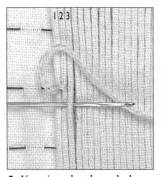

5. Keeping the thread above and the needle horizontal, take it from right to left through pleat 3, a quarter space below.

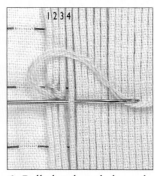

6. Pull the thread through. Keeping the thread above and the needle horizontal, take it from right to left through pleat 4.

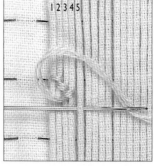

7. Pull the thread through to form a cable. Still keeping the thread above, take the needle from right to left through pleat 5 on the half space below.

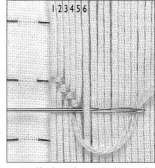

8. Pull the thread through. With the thread below the needle, take the needle from right to left through pleat 6.

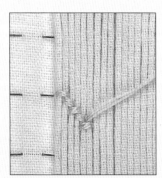

9. Pull the thread through to form an under cable.

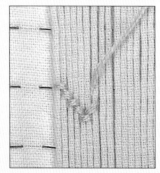

10. Keeping the thread below the needle, work a wave a quarter space above.

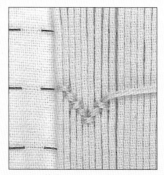

11. Still keeping the thread below the needle, work a cable.

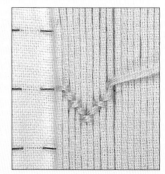

12. Still keeping the thread below the needle, work a wave up to the pleating row above.

STEPPED WAVE-CABLE COMBINATION... CONTINUED

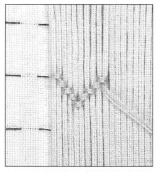

13. With the thread above the needle, work a cable stitch on the pleating row.

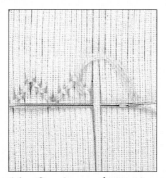

14. Continue alternating wave and cable stitches in the same manner to the end of the row.

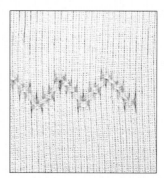

15. Work the last stitch as a cable stitch. Take the thread to the back of the fabric in the valley of the last stitch and end off.

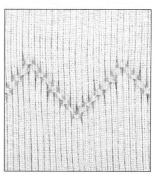

16. The number of stepped stitches can be varied but the method stays the same. Four-step wave/cable combination is shown here.

STEM STITCH

Stem stitch looks best when it is worked with a firm even tension.
It is very similar to outline stitch. For stem stitch the thread is kept below the needle for
all stitches and for outline stitch the thread is kept above the needle for all stitches.

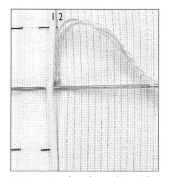

1. Secure the thread on the back of the fabric. Bring it to the front between pleats 1 and 2. Take the needle from right to left through the first pleat.

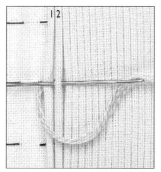

2. Pull the thread through. With the thread below the needle and the needle horizontal, take it from right to left through the second pleat.

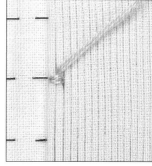

3. Pull the thread through until the stitch sits snugly against the pleat.

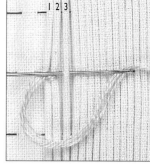

4. Keeping the thread below the needle, take the needle from right to left through the third pleat.

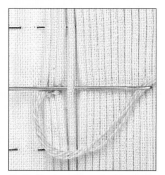

5. Pull the thread through. Keeping the thread below the needle, take the needle from right to left through the next pleat.

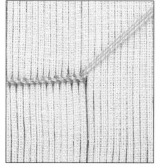

6. Pull the thread through. Continue to the end of the row in the same manner.

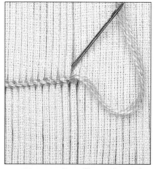

7. To end off, take the needle to the back of the fabric through the valley behind the last stem stitch.

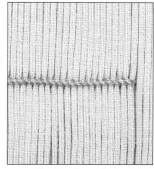

8. Pull the thread through and end off.

SATIN STITCH BAR

This accent stitch can be worked over any number of pleats but as it has no elasticity,
it is best worked after the smocking has been blocked.

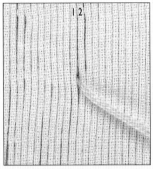

1. Secure the thread on the back of the fabric and bring it to the front between pleats 1 and 2.

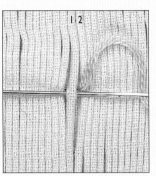

2. Take the needle from right to left through pleat 1. Pick up at least two thirds of the pleat and ensure the needle is horizontal.

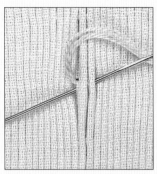

3. Pull the thread through. Take the needle from right to left through the required number of pleats. Angle the needle slightly so it emerges just below the thread.

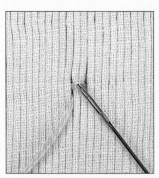

4. Gently pull the thread through. With the eye of the needle, straighten the pleats and loosen the stitch if necessary.

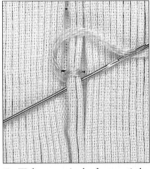

5. Take a stitch from right to left through the same pleats. Angle the needle to emerge directly below the previous stitch.

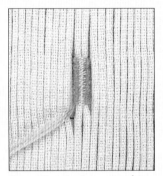

6. Continue working downwards in the same manner, keeping the stitches level and the tension even.

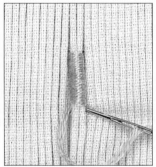

7. To end off, take the needle to the back of the fabric through the right hand side of the last pleat on the right.

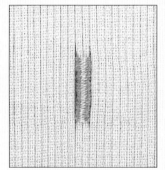

8. Pull the thread through and end off.

SURFACE EMBROIDERY ON PLEATS

SURFACE EMBROIDERY WILL REDUCE THE ELASTICITY OF THE SMOCKED PANEL.
BLOCK THE SMOCKING TO THE REQUIRED WIDTH BEFORE BEGINNING.

TAKE CARE WITH YOUR STITCH TENSION TO AVOID DISTORTING THE PLEATS.

PICK UP ONLY THE TIPS OF THE PLEATS FOR YOUR STITCHES TO KEEP THEM FROM
DISAPPEARING INTO THE VALLEYS.

AVOID CARRYING THREADS HORIZONTALLY ACROSS THE BACK OF THE SMOCKED FABRIC
FOR ANY GREAT DISTANCE AS THIS ALSO REDUCES THE ELASTICITY.

TWO-STEP TRELLIS

Trellis stitch is a very elastic stitch and is formed by working a combination
of cable and stepped stitches.

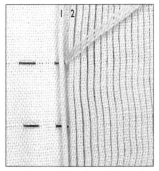

1. Secure the thread on the back of the fabric. Bring it to the front between pleats 1 and 2 on the upper pleating row.

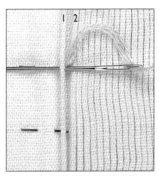

2. Take the needle from right to left through pleat 1 ready to begin stitching.

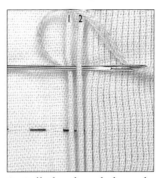

3. Pull the thread through. With the thread above the needle, take the needle from right to left through pleat 2.

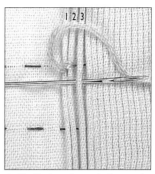

4. Pull the thread through. Keeping the thread above and the needle horizontal, take it from right to left through pleat 3 a quarter space below.

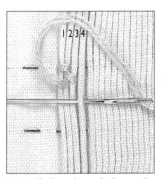

5. Pull the thread through. Keeping the thread above and the needle horizontal, take it from right to left through pleat 4, a quarter space below.

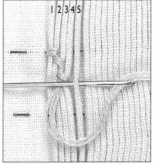

6. Pull the thread through. With the thread below the needle and still on the half space, take the needle from right to left through pleat 5.

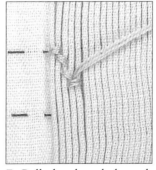

7. Pull the thread through to form a cable stitch.

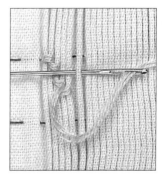

8. Keeping the thread below the needle, take the needle from right to left through the next pleat a quarter space above.

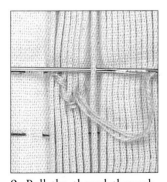

9. Pull the thread through. Keeping the thread below the needle, take the needle from right to left through the next pleat on the pleating row above.

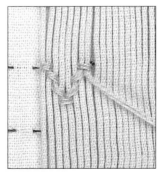

10. Pull the thread through. Work an over cable on the pleating row.

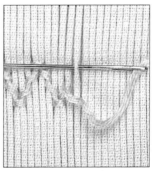

11. Continue working two steps down, under cable, two steps up, over cable across the row.

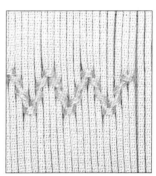

12. Work the last stitch as a cable stitch. Take the thread to the back of the fabric in the valley of the last stitch and end off.

FIVE-STEP TRELLIS

Trellis stitch can be worked with almost any number of stepped stitches.
To maintain consistent spacing when stitching the stepped stitches, use the pleating rows
as your guide, not the previous stitches.

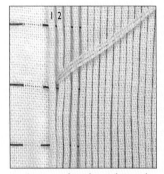

1. Secure the thread on the back of the fabric. Bring it to the front between pleats 1 and 2 on the pleating row.

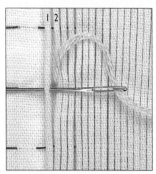

2. Take the needle from right to left through pleat 1 ready to begin stitching.

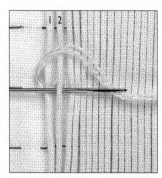

3. Pull the thread through. With the thread above the needle, take the needle from right to left through pleat 2.

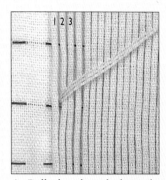

4. Pull the thread through. Keeping the thread above and the needle horizontal, take it from right to left through pleat 3, a fifth of the way to the next pleating row below.

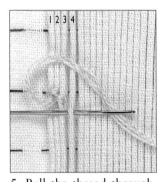

5. Pull the thread through. Keeping the thread above and the needle horizontal, take it from right to left through pleat 4, two fifths of the way to the pleating row below.

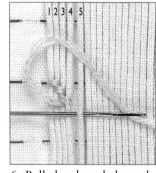

6. Pull the thread through. Keeping the thread above and the needle horizontal, take it from right to left through pleat 5, three fifths of the way to the pleating row below.

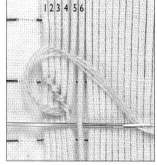

7. Pull the thread through. Keeping the thread above and the needle horizontal, take it from right to left through pleat 6, four fifths of the way to the pleating row below.

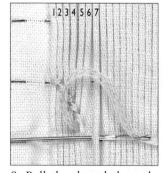

8. Pull the thread through. Keeping the thread above and the needle horizontal, take it from right to left through pleat 7, on the pleating row below.

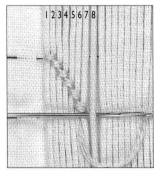

9. Pull the thread through. With the thread below the needle and still on the pleating row, take the needle from right to left through pleat 8.

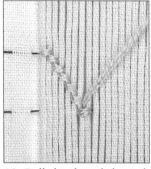

10. Pull the thread through to form an under cable.

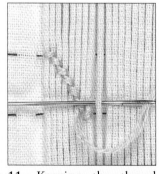

11. Keeping the thread below the needle, take the needle from right to left through the next pleat a fifth of the way up to the pleating row above.

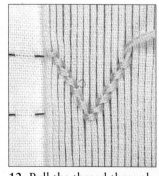

12. Pull the thread through. Keeping the thread below the needle, work four more stepped stitches a fifth of a space apart.

FIVE-STEP TRELLIS... CONTINUED

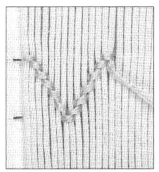

13. Work an over cable on the pleating row.

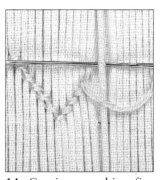

14. Continue working five steps down, under cable, five steps up, over cable across the row.

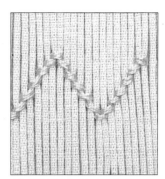

15. Work the last stitch as a cable stitch. Take the thread to the back of the fabric in the valley of the last stitch and end off.

BEADED TRELLIS

The trellis stitch is worked in exactly the same manner but a bead is threaded onto the needle before working each cable stitch. Do not add beads to stitches that are likely to come within the seam allowance.

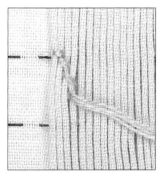

1. Work two-step trellis following steps 1 - 5 on page 107.

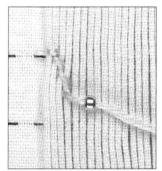

2. Slip a bead onto the needle and push it down the thread towards the fabric.

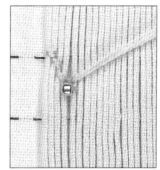

3. Work an under cable.

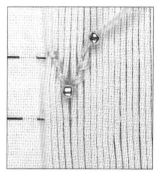

4. Work two-step trellis up to the upper pleating row. Slip a bead onto the needle.

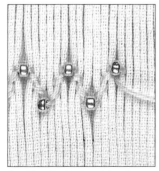

5. Continue working two-step trellis across the row, slipping a bead onto the needle before working each over and under cable.

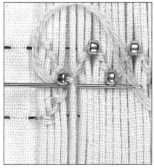

6. Begin a second trellis row. When the cable stitch butts the previous row, do not slip a bead onto the needle.

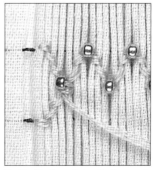

7. Pull the thread through as before, ensuring the cable sits snugly against the cable stitch of the previous row.

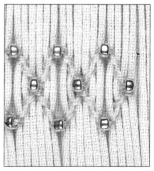

8. Continue to the end of the row, finishing with a cable stitch. Take the needle to the back of the fabric in the valley of the last stitch and end off.

VAN DYKE STITCH

Van Dyke stitch is one of the oldest smocking stitches and is very strong.
It is also very elastic and uses a lot of thread as each pleat is stitched twice.

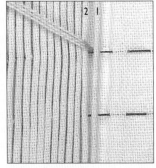

1. Secure the thread on the back of the fabric on the right hand side. Bring it to the front between the first and second pleats.

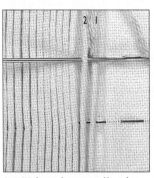

2. Take the needle from right to left through the second pleat, ready to begin stitching.

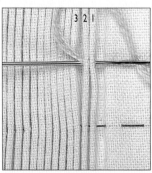

3. Pull the thread through. With the thread above the needle, take the needle from right to left through pleats 1 and 2.

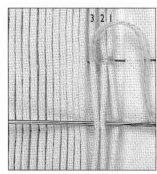

4. Pull the thread through. Keeping the thread above the needle, take the needle from right to left through pleats 2 and 3 on the pleating row below.

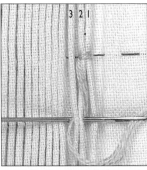

5. Pull the thread through. With the thread below the needle, take the needle from right to left through pleats 2 and 3 once more.

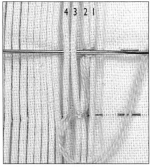

6. Pull the thread through. Keeping the thread below the needle, take the needle from right to left through pleats 3 and 4 on the pleating row above.

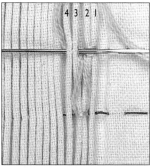

7. Pull the thread through. With the thread above the needle, take the needle from right to left through pleats 3 and 4 once more.

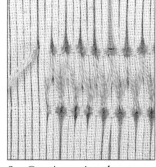

8. Continue in the same manner to the end of the row.

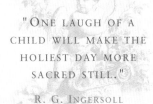

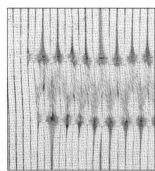

9. End with a horizontal stitch. Take the needle through the right hand side of the last used pleat and to the back of the fabric.

10. Pull the thread through and end off.

TWO-STEP VAN DYKE STITCH

This stitch is a variation of the traditional Van Dyke stitch.
The same method can be used to work multiple steps.

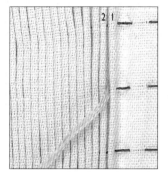

1. Secure the thread on the back of the fabric. Bring it to the front between pleats 1 and 2 on the right hand side.

2. Take the needle and thread from right to left through pleat 2 ready to begin stitching.

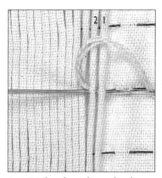

3. With the thread above the needle, take the needle from right to left through pleats 1 and 2.

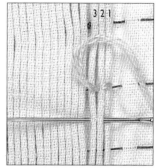

4. Pull the thread through. Keeping the thread above, take the needle from right to left through pleats 2 and 3, halfway to the next pleating row.

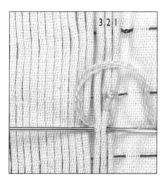

5. Pull the thread through. Still keeping the thread above, take the needle from right to left through pleats 2 and 3 once more.

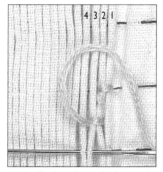

6. Pull the thread through. Still keeping the thread above, take the needle from right to left through pleats 3 and 4 on the pleating row below.

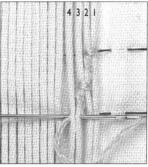

7. Pull the thread through. With the thread below the needle, take the needle from right to left through pleats 3 and 4 once more.

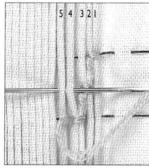

8. Pull the thread through. Keeping the thread below, take the needle from right to left through pleats 4 and 5 on the half space above.

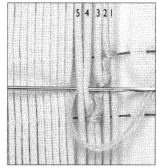

9. Pull the thread through. Keeping the thread below. Take the needle from right to left through pleats 4 and 5 again.

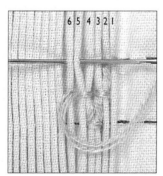

10. Pull the thread through. Still with the thread below, take the needle from right to left through pleats 5 and 6 on the first pleating row.

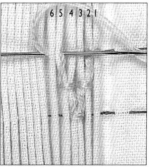

11. Pull the thread through. With the thread above the needle, take the needle from right to left through pleats 5 and 6 again.

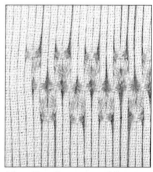

12. Continue working to the end of the row in the same manner. End off as for single Van Dyke stitch.

UKRAINE

At the time of the baptism parents are not supposed to go to the church. The Godparents take the child then bring him or her back. The Godmother brings 2-3 metres of cloth, known as a kryzhma She accepts the infant into the cloth once he or she is baptized. The Godfather pays the priest.

ESTONIA

A child's name could not be uttered until after it was baptized to protect it from attack from inimical forces. Some believe that if the child's name is spoken before the ceremony, he or she will grow up to be a thief.

ORKNEY ISLANDS

Pregnancy was concealed to avoid attracting the attention of trows or fairy folk. It is also considered extremely unlucky to prepare for the coming of a new baby - any such activity might alert the ever-present trows to the woman's condition. During pregnancy a knife and a bible were placed under the woman's bed. After the birth these two objects were transferred to the baby's cradle. Three feasts were held to celebrate the birth of the child. The first was the 'Blidemaet' (joyfood). The Blidemaet was usually scones and ale and was served to visiting families and neighbours who called to view the baby and congratulate the mother.

The second feast was the 'Fitten Feast' and was a private meal for the child's immediate family and marked the return 'to the fire' - the time when she was able to resume her daily household chores. The third and final feast was the 'Cirsenin Feast'. This was celebrated immediately after the baptism which usually took place within two weeks of the birth and most often within the first week. Any child who died in Orkney without being Christened could not be buried within the consecrated ground of the church.

If a girl and boy are to be Christened at the same ceremony the boy must be Christened first or the girl is doomed to grow a beard while the boy will remain beardless.

ISRAEL

An Israelite was never baptized by water. They were born under the terms of the covenant God made with Abraham (Genesis 15:1-12). But Gentiles who desired to become identified with the Jewish people entered into the water as an outward symbol of an internal commitment of faith in Jehovah as their one and only living God.

When they come to the water, let the water be pure and flowing.

And they shall put off their clothes.

And they shall baptize the little children first.

And if they can answer for themselves, let them answer.

But if they cannot, let their parents answer or someone from their family.

HIPPOLYTUS, 215AD

Christening mug

Construction

GENERAL INSTRUCTIONS

CUTTING OUT

Trace the pattern pieces onto lightweight interfacing or tracing paper, transferring all pattern markings. Where pattern pieces are not provided, cut the pieces according to the measurements given. Cut out all pattern pieces following the appropriate cutting layouts.

MAKING PIPING

Join the bias strips by placing the ends of two strips right sides together and at right angles to each other. Stitch diagonally across the overlapping ends (*diag 1*).

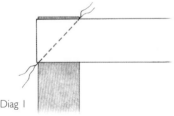

Diag 1

Trim the seam to 6mm ($1/4$") and press open. Continue joining strips until you have one long length of bias.

Lay the piping cord along the centre of the bias strip on the wrong side. Matching raw edges, fold the fabric over the cord. Stitch close to the cord (*diag 2*).

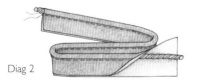

Diag 2

Trim the piping heading to the same width as the seam allowance on the garment.

BLOCKING SMOCKING

Remove the pleating threads except for the top holding row. With the right side uppermost, place the smocking onto a padded surface such as an ironing board. Pin to fit the blocking guide, ensuring the pleats are straight (*diag 3*).

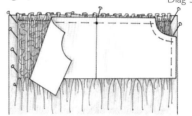

Diag 3

Steam, ensuring the iron does not touch the smocking. Alternatively, dampen by spraying with a water atomizer. Leave pinned until dry.

FRENCH SEAM

Pin the pieces wrong sides together. Stitch 6mm ($1/4$") from the raw edge. Trim the seam to 3mm ($1/8$") and press (*diag 4*).

With right sides together, fold the fabric along the seam and press. Stitch again, enclosing the raw edges (*diag 5*).

Press the seam towards the back.

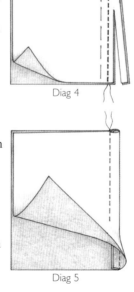

Diag 4

Diag 5

MAKING A PIPED COLLAR

Fuse interfacing to the wrong side of the collar. Cut a length of piping to fit the outer edge of the collar. Trim the piping heading to 1cm ($3/8$") if necessary. Clip the heading at 5mm ($3/16$") intervals.

With raw edges even, pin the piping to the right side of the collar around the outer edge. Stitch (*diag 6*).

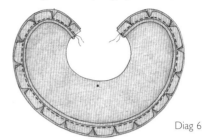

Diag 6

With right sides together and matching raw edges, pin and stitch the under collar to the piped collar, stitching between the corded edge of the piping and the previous stitchline. Stitch again, 3mm ($1/8$") away, within the seam allowance. Trim close to the second line of stitching (*diag 7*).

Diag 7

Turn to the right side and press. Baste the raw edges together.

CONTINUOUS LAP OR BOUND PLACKET

Starting at the upper edge, hand crease a fold for a short distance down the centre of the back skirt. Using a fabric marker, mark the fold with a line measuring the required length.

Staystitch along both sides of the line. Begin and end 3mm ($1/8$") away from the line at the upper edge and taper to a point at the lower edge (*diag 8*).

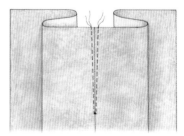

Diag 8

Cut down the line, taking care not to cut the stitching at the point. Spread the cut edges.

Place the placket and skirt right sides together, positioning the staystitching on the skirt just above the placket stitchline. Pin and stitch, taking care not to form pleats at the centre *(diag 9)*.

Diag 9

Press under the seam allowance on the remaining long edge of the placket. Fold the placket over the seam allowance to the wrong side. Pin the folded edge to the previous stitchline and hand stitch in place *(diag 10)*. Press.

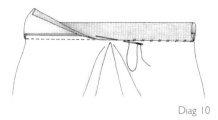

Diag 10

Fold the placket with right sides together and stitch across the lower end *(diag 11)*.

Fold the right hand side of the placket to the wrong side and baste at the upper edge. Leave the left hand side extended *(diag 12)*.

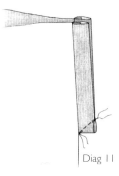

Diag 11

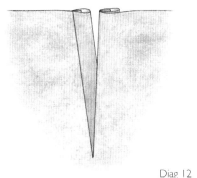

Diag 12

SETTING IN SLEEVES

With right sides together and matching raw edges, seams and pattern markings, pin a sleeve into the corresponding armhole. Pull up the gathering threads on the sleeve head to fit. Stitch *(diag 13)*. Trim the seam and neaten. Press.

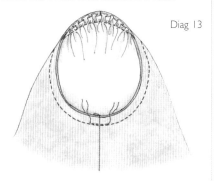

Diag 13

BINDING ARMHOLES

Turn under 5mm ($^3/_{16}$") on one end of the strip cut for the armhole binding. With the right side of the binding facing the inside of the armhole, align the folded end of the binding with the side seam. Pin the binding to the armhole, overlapping the binding by 5mm ($^3/_{16}$") at the side seam. Trim any excess binding. Stitch *(diag 14)*.

Trim the seam to 3mm ($^1/_8$"). Fold under 5mm ($^3/_{16}$") on the remaining raw edge of the binding. Fold the binding over the seam allowance. Hand stitch in place along the previous stitchline *(diag 15)*. Press.

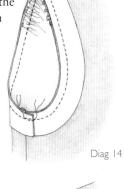

Diag 14

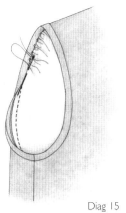

Diag 15

GOSSAMER

For full details and colour photos, see pages 8 - 17.

Sizes 3, 6 and 12 months

REQUIREMENTS

For full details, see pages 10, 11, 13 and 14.

PATTERN & CUTTING OUT

For full instructions, see liftout pattern sheet C.

PREPARATION & EMBROIDERY

For full instructions, see pages 11, 13 and 14.

CONSTRUCTION

All seam allowances are 1cm ($^3/_8$") unless otherwise specified.

THE GOWN

front

back

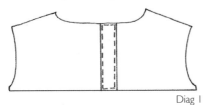

Diag I

TECHNIQUES USED

ATTACHING FLAT LACE TO
FLAT FABRIC, SEE PAGE 94

MAKING A CONTINUOUS LAP
PLACKET, SEE PAGES 114 - 115

FRENCH SEAM, SEE PAGE 114

SETTING IN SLEEVES,
SEE PAGE 115

1. Reinforcing the back yoke

With wrong sides together, press the back yoke foldlines. Position a strip of organza on the wrong side of the back yoke lining along the fold. Tack in place *(diag 1)*. Repeat on the remaining back yoke, ensuring you have a left and a right back yoke.

2. Shoulder seams

With right sides together and matching raw edges, pin and stitch the front yoke to the back yoke pieces at the shoulders. Repeat for the linings. Trim the seams and press towards the back *(diag 2)*.

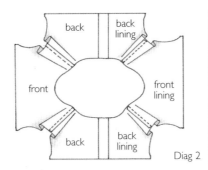

Diag 2

3. Neckline

Matching shoulder seams, fold the yoke and lining right sides together. Pin and stitch around the neckline *(diag 3)*.

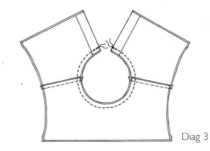

Diag 3

Stitch again 3mm ($1/8$") from the previous stitchline within the seam allowance. Trim the seam. Turn to the right side and press. The yoke and lining will now be treated as one layer. Tack the two pieces together around all raw edges.

4. Front skirt

Matching raw edges, place two upper skirt pieces together. Tack around all four sides. The two layers will be treated as one from now on.

Using the armhole cutting guide, cut out the armhole shaping from the two top corners *(diag 4)*.

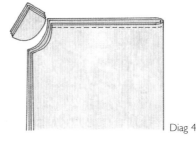

Diag 4

Mark the centre and stitch two rows of machine gathering across the top.

Cut a length of piping to fit the lower edge of the front yoke. With right sides together, pin and stitch the piping to the lower edge of the front yoke *(diag 5)*. Mark the centre.

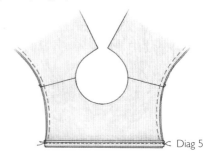

Diag 5

Pull up the skirt gathers to fit the front yoke. With right sides together and matching centre marks and armholes, pin the skirt to the yoke. With the yoke uppermost, stitch between the corded edge of the piping and the previous stitchline *(diag 6)*. Stitch again 3mm ($1/8$") from the previous stitching.

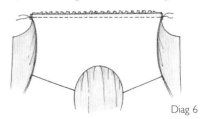

Diag 6

Trim the seam close to the second line of stitching and neaten. Press the seam towards the yoke.

5. Placket

Tack the remaining two upper skirt pieces together following the diagram and cut out the armhole shaping from the two top corners *(diag 7)*.

Diag 7

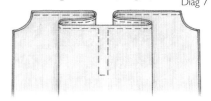

Marking a line measuring 9.5cm ($3 5/8$") from the upper edge of the skirt, make the placket following the instructions on pages 114 - 115.

6. Back skirt

Work two rows of machine gathering across each half of the skirt. Pull up the gathers to fit the back yoke. With right sides together and matching armhole edges and the finished edge of the yoke with the edge of the placket, pin the skirt to the yoke. Stitch *(diag 8)*.

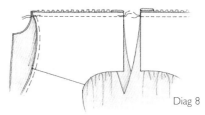

Diag 8

Stitch again 3mm (1/8") from the previous stitching. Trim the seam close to the second line of stitching and neaten. Press the seam towards the yoke.

7. Side seams

Using a fine French seam, pin and stitch the side seams (diag 9).

Diag 9

8. Sleeves

Join a piece of lace beading and lace edging following the instructions on page 94 (diag 10).

Diag 10

Find the two ribbon holes closest to the centre and mark.

Mark the centre of the lower edge of the sleeve. Matching centre marks, attach the lace to the lower edge of the sleeve following the instructions on page 97 (diag 11).

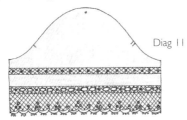

Diag 11

If necessary, trim excess lace from each end of the sleeve.

Cut a 50cm (19 5/8") length of ribbon and thread through the lace beading. Leave a long loop at the centre (diag 12).

Diag 12

The ends of the ribbon will be secured in the sleeve seam later.

Pin and tack a length of lace insertion to the right side of the sleeve, centred over the line indicated on the pattern. Stitch along the lace heading on each side using a zigzag stitch.

Stitch two rows of machine gathering across each sleeve head between the marks indicated on the pattern.

Stitch the underarm seam, including the lace, with a fine French seam (diag 13). Repeat for the second sleeve.

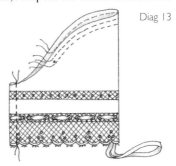

Diag 13

Set in the sleeves following the instructions on page 115.

9. Lower skirt

Using a fine French seam, join the two pieces of tulle for tier 1 so that you have one long piece (diag 14).

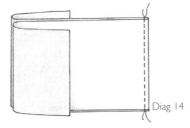

Diag 14

Press. Join together one length of lace beading and one length of lace insertion and attach to the lower edge of the tier in the same manner as the sleeves. Pin and stitch a length of lace insertion to the right side of the tier, 1.5cm (5/8") away from the upper edge of the lace beading (diag 15). Thread satin ribbon through the beading.

Diag 15

Aligning laces and using a fine French seam, join the ends of the tier to form a circle.

Assemble the three remaining tiers in the same manner.

10. Attaching the lower skirt

Matching upper edges and side seams, place all the tiers together. Tack around the upper edge. The four layers will be treated as one from now on.

With wrong sides together and matching side seams, pin and stitch the lower skirt to the upper skirt. Trim and grade the seam. Press the seam towards the lower skirt (diag 16).

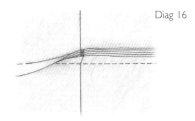

Diag 16

Join together the remaining lengths of lace beading and edging in the same manner as before. Thread the remaining piece of ribbon through the beading. Join the ends, forming a circle to fit around the seam between the upper and lower skirt. With the wrong side of the lace facing the right side of the skirt, position the circle of lace over the seam. Pin and stitch along both edges of the lace beading (diag 17). Press.

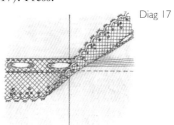

Diag 17

11. Finishing

Work two buttonholes on the right back yoke at the positions indicated on the pattern. Attach two buttons to the left back yoke to correspond. Remove the tacking from the back yoke reinforcing.

Cut the ends of the ribbon for the sleeve ties at an angle. Pull up the gathers and tie the ribbons into bows.

BONNET

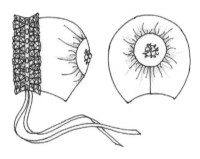

1. Centre back seam

With right sides together and matching raw edges, fold the bonnet piece in half. Stitch the centre back seam (*diag 1*).

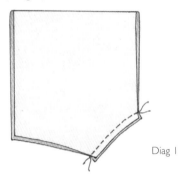

Diag 1

Trim the seam and press. Turn to the right side. Repeat for the bonnet lining.

2. Inserting the crown

Work two rows of machine gathering around the back opening of both the bonnet and bonnet lining. Fold the opening into quarters and mark each fold with the fabric marker. Unfold (*diag 2*).

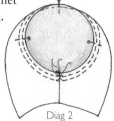

Diag 2

Mark the crown and crown lining into quarters in the same manner.

With right sides together and matching quarter marks, pin the bonnet to the crown. Pull up the gathers to fit. Stitch (*diag 3*).

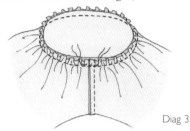

Diag 3

Stitch again 3mm ($^1/_8$") away from the previous stitchline within the seam allowance. Trim close to the second line of stitching. Press towards the crown.

Insert the crown lining into the bonnet lining in the same manner.

3. Joining the bonnet and lining

With right sides together and matching raw edges, pin the bonnet to the lining. Stitch around all sides leaving a 5cm (2") opening in the front for turning (*diag 4*).

Diag 4

Stitch again. Trim the seam, turn to the right side and press. Turn under the seam allowance along the opening. Hand stitch the opening closed.

4. Making the lace frill

Attach the length of lace insertion to the length of lace edging following the instructions on page 94. Cut the length of lace in half.

Gather and attach a piece of joined lace to each side of the lace beading following the instructions on page 96 (*diag 5*).

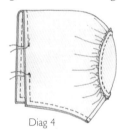

Diag 5

Thread the length of satin ribbon through the beading.

5. Attaching the lace frill

Pin the frill to the front of the bonnet so the edge of the lace beading aligns with the finished edge of the bonnet and the pattern in the beading is centred (*diag 6*). Leave 1cm ($^3/_8$") of lace extending at each end. Stitch along both sides of the beading.

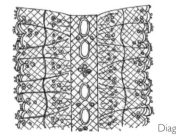

Diag 6

Fold the extension to the inside of the bonnet and press. Fold under the raw end of the frill and hand stitch in place (*diag 7*). Repeat at the other end.

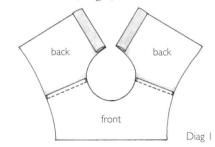

Diag 7

6. Finishing

Catch the bonnet and lining together along the crown seam with several hand stitches.

Work the embroidery on the crown following the instructions on page 14. Fashion two more ribbon flowers and attach one to each side of the bonnet, securing the ribbon ties at the same time.

PETTICOAT

1. Yoke

Using a fine French seam, join the front yoke to the back yoke at the shoulders. Press the seams towards the back.

Fold under 2cm ($^3/_4$") at the centre back opening on each half of the back yoke. Press. Fold under a further 2cm ($^3/_4$") on each half and press to form the button band (*diag 1*).

back

back

front

Diag 1

2. Front skirt

Using the armhole cutting guide for the gown, cut out the armhole shaping from the front skirt *(diag 2)*.

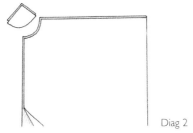

Diag 2

Stitch two rows of machine gathering across the top. Pull up the gathers to fit the front yoke. With right sides together and matching armhole and raw edges, pin and stitch the skirt to the yoke. Stitch again 5mm ($^3/_{16}$") from the previous stitching *(diag 3)*.

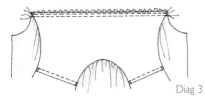

Diag 3

Trim the seam close to the second line of stitching and neaten. Press the seam towards the yoke.

3. Placket

Marking a line measuring 12cm (4") from the upper edge of the skirt, make the placket following the instructions on pages 114 - 115.

4. Back skirt

Cut out the armhole shaping in the same manner as the front skirt.

Work two rows of machine gathering across each half of the skirt. Pull up the gathers to fit the back yoke. With right sides together and matching armhole edges and the folded edge of the yoke with the edge of the placket, pin each half of the skirt to the corresponding back yoke. Wrap the button band around the skirt. Stitch *(diag 4)*.

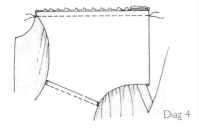

Diag 4

Stitch again 5mm ($^3/_{16}$") from the previous stitching. Trim the seam close to the second line of stitching and neaten. Press the seam towards the yoke.

5. Attaching lace to the neckline

Unfold the button bands at the neckline. Cut a length of lace edging to fit the neckline including the back button bands. Place the wrong side of the lace edging to the right side of the yoke, aligning the scalloped edge of the lace with the raw edge of the fabric. Stitch along the lace heading *(diag 5)*.

Diag 5

button band

Clip the curve at 6mm ($^1/_4$") intervals. Fold back the fabric behind the lace and press. Zigzag over the first line of stitching *(diag 6)*.

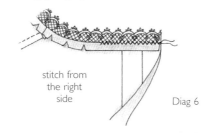

stitch from the right side

Diag 6

Trim away the excess fabric. Refold the button band and hand stitch in place.

6. Attaching lace to the armholes

Cut two lengths of lace edging to fit the armhole. Attach lace edging to each armhole in the same manner as the neckline.

7. Hem and side seams

Stitch one side seam using a fine French seam.

Adjust the length of the petticoat to suit the length of the gown. Stitch lace edging to the lower edge of the skirt using the same method as the neckline.

Complete the remaining side seam with a fine French seam. Press the seams towards the back.

---

8. Finishing

Work two buttonholes on the right back button band at the positions indicated on the pattern. Attach two buttons to the left back button band to correspond.

DELIGHT

For full details and colour photos, see pages 18 - 25.

Sizes 3, 6 and 12 months

REQUIREMENTS

For full details, see page 20.

PATTERN & CUTTING OUT

For full instructions, see liftout pattern sheet C.

PREPARATION & PLEATING

For full instructions, see page 20.

SMOCKING

For full instructions, see pages 21 - 23.

PREPARATION & EMBROIDERY

For full instructions, see pages 21 - 22.

CONSTRUCTION

All seam allowances are 1cm ($^3/_8$") unless otherwise specified.

TECHNIQUES USED

BLOCKING SMOCKING, SEE PAGE 114

FRENCH SEAM, SEE PAGE 114

SETTING IN SLEEVES, SEE PAGE 115

BINDING THE ARMHOLES, SEE PAGE 115

front

back

1. Blocking and shaping

Block the smocking following the instructions on page 114. Using a narrow zigzag or short straight stitch, stitch just inside the marked lines around the neckline and armholes on the front. Cut along the marked lines *(diag 1)*.

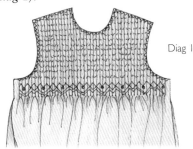

Diag 1

Place the two back overskirt pieces right sides together. Using the back armhole cutting guide, mark and cut out the armhole shaping from one corner through both layers *(diag 2)*. Repeat for the back underskirt.

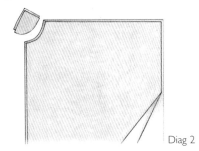

Diag 2

2. Preparing the back yoke

Place the wrong side of one organza back yoke onto the right side of one dupion back yoke interlining. Baste the two layers together around all edges *(diag 3)*.

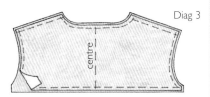

Diag 3

centre

These pieces will be treated as a single layer from now on. Repeat for the remaining two back yoke pieces.

3. Shoulder seams

With right sides together and matching raw edges, pin and stitch the front to the back yoke pieces at the shoulders. Repeat for the linings.

Press the yoke seams towards the back and the lining seams open *(diag 4)*.

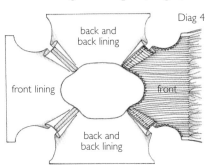

Diag 4

back and
back lining

front lining

front

back and
back lining

Finish the lower edge of the front yoke lining with a narrow hem.

4. Forming the back skirt button bands

On each back overskirt opening edge, fold under 2.5cm (1") and press. Fold under a further 2.5cm (1") and press. Tack. Pin and baste at the upper edge. Repeat for the underskirt.

Stitch close to the inner folded edge on each underskirt button band *(diag 5)*.

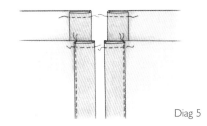

Diag 5

5. Attaching the back skirt

Matching raw edges and back opening edges, place the wrong side of one overskirt onto the right side of the corresponding underskirt and pin. The two layers are treated as one while attaching them to the back yoke. Stitch two rows of machine gathering across the top *(diag 6)*.

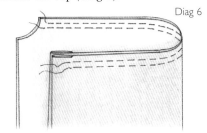

Diag 6

Pull up the gathers to fit the back yoke. Do not gather the button band. Repeat for the remaining back skirt.

With right sides together and matching raw edges, pin each side of the back skirt to the corresponding back yoke. Ensure the linings are out of the way and stitch in place *(diag 7)*.

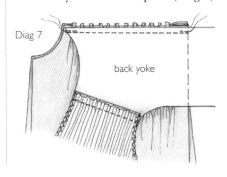

Diag 7

back yoke

Fold the back yoke linings around the skirt, sandwiching the skirt between. Pin and stitch along the previous stitchline *(diag 8)*.

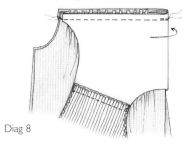

Diag 8

Trim the seams, turn to the right side and press.

6. Neck binding

Matching shoulder seams and raw edges, fold the lining to the inside. Baste the raw edges together around the neckline.

With wrong sides together, fold the neck binding in half along the length and press. Matching raw edges, pin the doubled binding to the neckline, stretching the binding slightly. Leave 5mm (³/₁₆") extending beyond the back opening edges. Stitch *(diag 9)*.

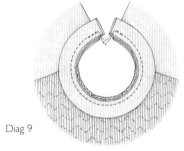

Diag 9

Stitch again, 5mm (³/₁₆") away from the seam. Trim very close to the second row of stitching.

Fold in the extended ends of the binding and then firmly fold the binding over the seam allowance to the wrong side. Pin and hand stitch the binding in place *(diag 10)*.

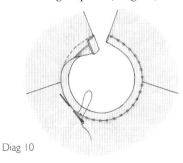

Diag 10

7. Side seams

Matching raw edges and shoulder seams, pin and tack the lining to the yoke around the armholes.

The side seams for the overskirt and underskirt are stitched separately. With wrong sides together and matching raw edges, pin the front and back overskirts together at the sides. Stitch using a fine French seam *(diag 11)*.

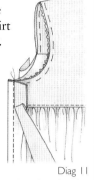

Diag 11

Press the seams towards the back. Repeat for the underskirt side seams. Tack the overskirt and underskirt together at the underarms.

8. Sleeves

Stitch two rows of machine gathering across each sleeve head between the marks indicated on the pattern. Repeat on the lower edge of each sleeve. Pull up the gathers on the lower edge to fit the sleeve binding.

With wrong sides together, fold the sleeve binding in half along the length and press. Matching raw edges, pin the doubled binding to the right side of the sleeve. Stitch *(diag 12)*.

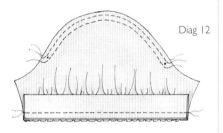

Diag 12

Stitch again 5mm (³/₁₆") away from the seam. Trim very close to the second row of stitching.

Pin and stitch the underarm seams, including the binding, using a fine French seam *(diag 13)*. Press.

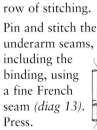

Diag 13

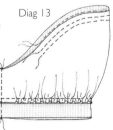

Firmly fold the binding over the seam allowance to the wrong side. Pin and hand stitch the binding to the previous stitchline *(diag 14)*.

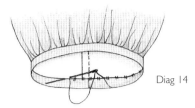

Diag 14

Set in the sleeves following the instructions on page 115.

9. Hemline scallops

Unfold the button bands on the overskirt at the lower edge. Using a fine French seam, stitch the back skirt scallop pieces to the front skirt scallop piece at the sides. Press the seams towards the back.

Beginning at the centre front and using the scallop template, mark scallops across the entire width of the fabric *(diag 15)*.

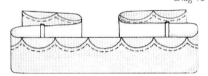

Diag 15

With wrong sides together and matching seams, pin the scallops to the lower edge of the overskirt. Fold the ends of the scallops level with the back opening edges of the overskirt and press. Stitch along the lower edge *(diag 16)*.

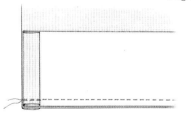

Diag 16

Trim and press the scallops to the right side of the overskirt.

Cut out the scallops along the upper edge leaving a 5mm (³/₁₆") seam allowance. Fold under the seam allowance and pin in place, clipping the curves as you go. At the peaks, fold under one side and then the other to make a crisp point *(diag 17)*.

Diag 17

121

Stitch in place close to the folded edge. Press. Refold the button bands at the lower edge and press. Hand stitch the button band to the hem (diag 18).

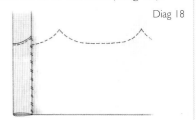

Diag 18

10. Underskirt hem

Fold under 3.5cm (1 $^1/_8$") on the lower edge of the underskirt and press. Fold under a further 3.5cm (1 $^1/_8$") and press. Pin and hand stitch in place.

11. Embroidery

Transfer and work the embroidery designs following the instructions on pages 21 - 22.

12. Finishing

Matching folded edges, tack the overskirt to the underskirt at the back opening edges. These will be treated as one layer for working the buttonholes and attaching the buttons.

Stitch two buttonholes on the right back yoke at the positions indicated on the pattern. Stitch five more button-holes on the upper section of the right back button band spacing them approx-imately 8cm (3 $^1/_8$") apart. Attach buttons to the left back yoke and skirt to correspond. Attach the snap fastener to the ends of the neck binding.

STARDUST

For full details and colour photos, see pages 26 - 33.

Sizes 3, 6 and 12 months

REQUIREMENTS

For full details, see pages 28 - 31.

PATTERN & CUTTING OUT

For full instructions, see liftout pattern sheet D.

PREPARATION & EMBROIDERY

For full instructions, see pages 28 - 31.

CONSTRUCTION

All seam allowances are 1cm ($^3/_8$") unless otherwise specified.

GOWN

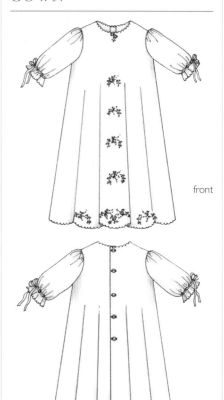

front

back

TECHNIQUES USED

FRENCH SEAM, SEE PAGE 114

BINDING ARMHOLES, SEE PAGE 115

ATTACHING FLAT FABRIC TO ENTREDEUX, SEE PAGE 95

SETTING IN SLEEVES, SEE PAGE 115

1. Joining the front to the back

Using fine French seams, stitch the front to the back at the shoulders and sides (diag 1). Press.

Diag I

2. Button bands

On each back opening edge, fold under 2.5cm (1") and press. Fold under a further 2.5cm (1") and press. Tack. Hand stitch the button bands in place (diag 2). Press.

Diag 2

3. Working the scallops and embroidery

Machine stitch the scallops and work all embroidery following the instructions on pages 28 - 29.

4. Sleeves

Set in the sleeves without trimming and neatening the seams, following the instructions on page 115.

Bind the armholes following the instructions on page 115. Press.

5. Finishing

Stitch five buttonholes on the upper section of the right back button band at the positions indicated on the pattern. Attach buttons to the left back button band to correspond.

Cut the narrow satin ribbon in half and cut the ends at an angle. Beginning at the centre, thread a length through the eyelets on each sleeve and tie into a bow.

PETTICOAT

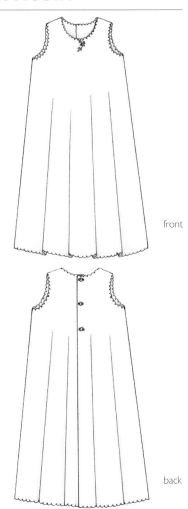

front

back

1. Shoulder seams

Using fine French seams, stitch the front to the back at the shoulders *(diag 1)*. Press.

Diag I

2. Button bands

See step 2 of the gown.

3. Neckline and armholes

Machine stitch the scallops around the neckline and armholes following the instructions on page 30.

4. Side seams

Using fine French seams, stitch the front to the back at the sides *(diag 2)*.

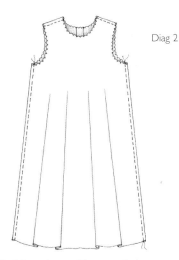

Diag 2

5. Working the scallops and embroidery

Machine stitch the hem scallops and work all embroidery following the instructions on pages 28 and 30.

6. Finishing

Stitch three buttonholes on the right back button band at the positions indicated on the pattern. Attach buttons to the left back button band to correspond.

BONNET

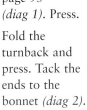

1. Shaping the bonnet

Cut a piece of entredeux the same length as the centre back seam and insert into the seam following the instructions on page 95 *(diag 1)*. Press.

Fold the turnback and press. Tack the ends to the bonnet *(diag 2)*.

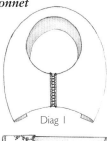

Diag I

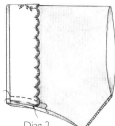

Diag 2

Cut a length of entredeux to fit the lower edge of the bonnet. Attach one edge of the entredeux to the lower edge of the bonnet, following the instructions on page 95. Trim off the remaining heading of the entredeux *(diag 3)*. Press.

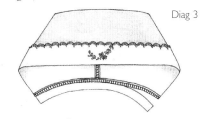

Diag 3

2. Inserting the crown

Using the centre back seam as one mark, fold the opening into quarters and mark each fold with the fabric marker. Unfold *(diag 4)*.

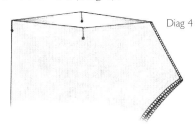

Diag 4

Work two rows of machine gathering around the back opening of the bonnet.

With right sides together and matching quarter marks, pin the bonnet to the crown *(diag 5)*.

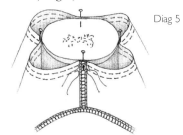

Diag 5

Ensure the embroidery is the correct orientation. Pull up the gathers to fit. Stitch *(diag 6)*.

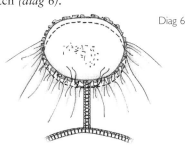

Diag 6

Trim the seam to 2 - 3 mm ($^1/_8$"). Press towards the crown.

Staystitch around the crown lining along the stitchline. Press under the seam allowance, ensuring that the staystitching is just to the underside. Trim the seam allowance to 2 - 3 mm ($^1/_8$"). Matching quarter marks and with wrong sides together, pin the crown lining to the crown. Hand stitch in place (diag 7). Press.

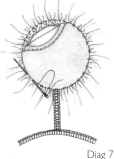

Diag 7

3. Attaching the ties

Cut two pieces of the wide satin ribbon, each 29cm (11 $^3/_8$") long for the ribbon rosettes and two pieces, each 40cm (15 $^3/_4$") long for the ties.

Beginning and ending 1cm ($^3/_8$") from the ends, mark each piece of ribbon for the rosettes at 3cm (1 $^1/_8$") intervals.

Using a tiny running stitch, stitch across the ribbon as shown (diag 8).

Diag 8

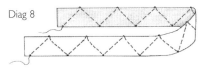

Pull up the thread to gather the ribbon and tie off securely. Place the ends right sides together and hand stitch (diag 9).

Diag 9

Fold under the raw ends and secure on the back of the petal. Catch the ends of the petals together in the centre (diag 10). Make the second rosette in the same manner.

Diag 10

Position the end of one ribbon tie on the turnback at the position indicated on the pattern. Place a rosette over the end of the ribbon. Secure the rosette and ribbon tie with several hand stitches that go through all layers. Repeat on the remaining side.

CHERUB

For full details and colour photos, see pages 34 - 39.

Sizes 3, 6 and 12 months

REQUIREMENTS

For full details, see page 36.

PATTERN & CUTTING OUT

For full details, see liftout pattern sheet B.

PREPARATION & EMBROIDERY

For full instructions, see pages 36 - 37.

CONSTRUCTION

All seam allowances are 1cm ($^3/_8$") unless otherwise specified.

TECHNIQUES USED

MAKING PIPING, SEE PAGE 114

ATTACHING FLAT FABRIC TO ENTREDEUX, SEE PAGE 95

MAKING A PIPED COLLAR, SEE PAGE 114

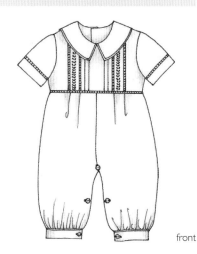

front

back

1. Making piping

Make the piping following the instructions on page 114.

2. Reinforcing the back bodice

Fold the back bodice pieces in half and press the back opening foldlines. Fuse the interfacing onto the wrong side of the back bodice linings, aligning one long edge with the pressed foldline (diag 1).

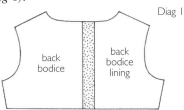

Diag 1

back bodice

back bodice lining

3. Shoulder seams

With right sides together and matching raw edges, pin and stitch the front bodice to the back bodice pieces at the shoulders. Repeat for the lining. Press the seams open (diag 2).

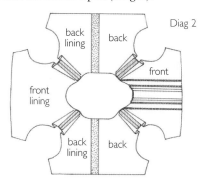

Diag 2

back lining

back

front

front lining

back lining

back

4. Collar

Make the collar following the instructions on page 114. Make the second half of the collar in the same manner.

Secure the collar pieces together on the stitchline at the centre front *(diag 3)*.

Diag 3

Matching raw edges, centre fronts and centre backs and with the under collar facing the right side of the bodice, pin and tack the collar to the bodice *(diag 4)*. Keep the lining out of the way.

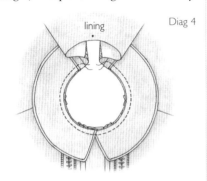

lining

Diag 4

With right sides together and matching raw edges and seams at the neckline, place the lining over the bodice. The collar is sandwiched between. Pin through all layers. Stitch around the neckline, beginning and ending off securely *(diag 5)*. Trim the seam and clip at approximately 1cm (³/₈") intervals.

Diag 5

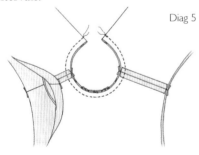

Open out the lining. Keeping the bodice out of the way, under-stitch around the neckline close to the seam, stitching through the lining and the seam allowance beneath *(diag 6)*.

Diag 6

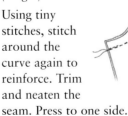

Fold the lining to the inside and press.

5. Pants back

Neaten the outer and lower edges of each facing piece. With right sides together and matching raw edges, pin and stitch a facing to each side of the back opening, ending at the marked point *(diag 7)*.

Diag 7

Trim the seam up to the marked point and clip into the corners. Trim off the outer corners *(diag 8)*.

Turn to the right side and press.

Diag 8

With right sides together and keeping the ends of the facing free of the seam, stitch the two back pieces together beginning at the marked point *(diag 9)*.

Using tiny stitches, stitch around the curve again to reinforce. Trim and neaten the seam. Press to one side.

Diag 9

Place the lower ends of the back opening right over left. Beginning and ending off securely, topstitch across the diagonal edge *(diag 10)*. Press.

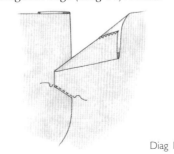

Diag 10

6. Centre front and side seams

With right sides together, stitch the two front pants pieces together at the centre front *(diag 11)*.

Diag 11

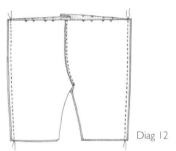

Reinforce the curve in the same manner as on the back. Trim and neaten the seam. Press to one side.

With right sides together, stitch the front pants to the back pants at the sides *(diag 12)*. Trim and neaten the seams. Press towards the back.

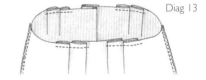

Diag 12

7. Attaching the pants

Fold the pleats in the upper edge of the pants and pin.

Matching centre fronts, side seams and the back bodice foldlines to the seamed edge of the pants facings, check that the upper edge of the pants is the same size as the lower edge of the bodice. Staystitch the pleats in place *(diag 13)*.

Diag 13

Cut a length of entredeux to fit the upper edge of the pants, including both sides of the back opening facing. With right sides together, attach the entredeux to the lower edge of the bodice following the instructions on page 95 *(diag 14)*.

Diag 14

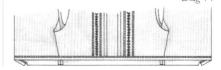

125

Matching all the points as before, attach the upper edge of the pants to the remaining heading of the entre-deux in the same manner. Ensure the bodice lining is out of the way *(diag 15)*.

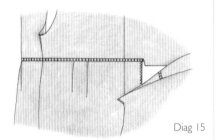

Diag 15

8. Securing the lining

With right sides together and matching raw edges, pin and stitch the front bodice lining to the back bodice lining at the sides. Press the seams open.

Matching raw edges and seams, pin and tack the lining to the bodice around the armholes. Fold under 5mm (³/₁₆") on the lower edge of the bodice lining and press. Matching seams, pin and hand stitch the lining to the lower edge of the entredeux *(diag 16)*.

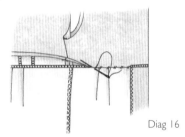

Diag 16

9. Sleeves

Cut off the lower section of each sleeve along the marked line for the sleeve band. Cut two lengths of entredeux to fit across the lower edge of the sleeve. Using the entredeux, reattach the sleeve bands to the sleeves following the instructions on page 95. *(diag 17)*.

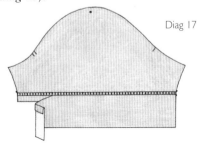

Diag 17

Stitch two rows of machine gathering across the head of the sleeves between the marks indicated on the pattern.

With right sides together, stitch the underarm seam including the sleeve band *(diag 18)*.

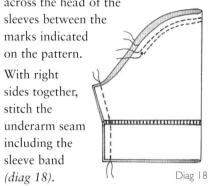

Diag 18

Trim and neaten the seam. Press.

Press under 5mm (³/₁₆") on the lower edge of the sleeve band. Fold half the band to the inside and pin the folded edge to align with the upper seam of the entredeux. Hand stitch in place.

Matching seams and markings, pin each sleeve into the corresponding armhole. Pull up the gathering threads, easing the sleeve to fit the armhole. Ensure no pleats form across the head of the sleeves. Stitch *(diag 19)*.

Trim and neaten the seams. Press.

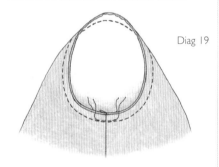

Diag 19

10. Inside leg button bands

With wrong sides together, fold the inside leg button bands in half and press. Matching centres and raw edges, pin and stitch one band to the right side of the front inside leg edge *(diag 20)*.

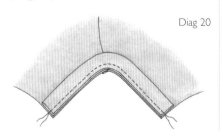

Diag 20

Trim the seam. Understitch along the band *(diag 21)*.

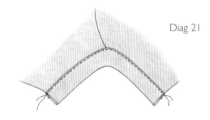

Diag 21

Fold the band to the inside and press. Tack in place.

Attach the remaining button band to the back inside leg edge in the same manner.

11. Lower leg bands

Cut two lengths of piping to fit the long edge of the lower leg band. Fuse interfacing to the upper half of both bands. Pin and stitch piping to the upper edge of the interfaced section *(diag 22)*.

Diag 22

Stitch two rows of machine gathering across the lower edge of the legs. Do not include the inside leg button bands.

With right sides together and leaving 1cm (³/₈") of the band extending at both ends, pin the leg band to the lower edge of the leg. Pull up the gathers to fit, positioning the pants side seam in the centre of the leg band. Stitch between the corded edge of the piping and the previous stitchline *(diag 23)*.

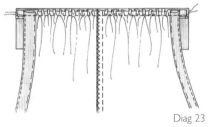

Diag 23

Trim the seam and press towards the band.

Press under the seam allowance on the lower edge of the band and trim to 5mm (³/₁₆"). With right sides together, fold the band in half. Stitch the ends *(diag 24)*.

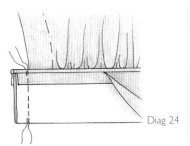

Diag 24

Clip the corners, turn to the right side and press.

Position the folded edge of the band to align with the previous stitching and hand stitch in place *(diag 25)*. Press.

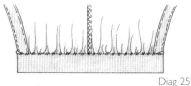

Diag 25

12. Finishing

Stitch the buttonholes on the right back bodice and lower leg bands at the positions indicated on the pattern. Stitch five evenly spaced buttonholes along the front inside leg button band *(diag 26)*. Attach the buttons to correspond.

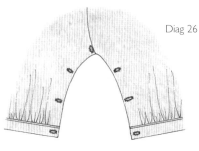

Diag 26

CARESS

For full details and colour photos, see pages 40 - 41.

Sizes 3, 6 and 12 months

REQUIREMENTS

For full details, see page 42.

PATTERN & CUTTING OUT

For full instructions, see liftout pattern sheet B and pages 42 - 43.

PREPARATION & PLEATING

For full instructions, see page 43.

SMOCKING

For full instructions, see pages 43 - 45.

PREPARATION & EMBROIDERY

For full instructions, see page 44.

CONSTRUCTION

All seam allowances are 1cm (³/8") unless otherwise specified.

TECHNIQUES USED

ATTACHING FLAT LACE TO FLAT FABRIC, SEE PAGE 94

FRENCH SEAM, SEE PAGE 114

front

back

1. Side seams

Using a French seam, pin and stitch the underarm and side seams *(diag 1)*. Press the seams towards the back.

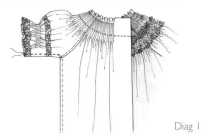

Diag 1

2. Hem

At the lower edge, fold under 4.5cm (1 ³/4") and press. Fold under a further 4.5cm (1 ³/4") and press. Stitch the hem in place *(diag 2)*. Press.

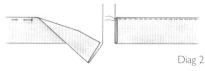

Diag 2

3. Button bands

Fold under 2.5cm (1") along one centre back edge and press. Fold again for 2.5cm (1") and press *(see diag 3)*.

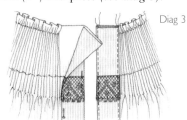

Diag 3

127

Topstitch down both sides of the button band 3mm (¹/8") in from the folded edges (diag 3). Repeat for the remaining button band.

4. Binding the neckline

With wrong sides together, fold the binding in half along the length and press. Matching raw edges, pin the doubled binding to the right side of the neckline, stretching the binding slightly. Leave 1cm (³/8") extending beyond the back opening foldlines. Stitch (diag 4). Press.

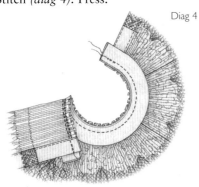

Diag 4

Trim the seam to 4mm (³/16"). Fold in the ends of the binding level with the back edges. Fold the binding over the seam allowance to the wrong side. Pin and handstitch the binding in place (diag 5). Press.

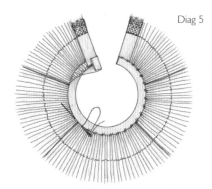

Diag 5

5. Finishing

Stitch two vertical buttonholes on the upper end of the right back button band, spacing them approximately 4cm (1¹/2") apart. Stitch a further three buttonholes 11.5cm (4¹/2") apart, below the first two.

Attach buttons on the left back button band to correspond.

GRACE

For full details and colour photos, see pages 48 - 57.

Sizes 3, 6 and 12 months

REQUIREMENTS

For full details, see pages 50, 51, 54 and 55.

PATTERN & CUTTING OUT

For full details, see liftout pattern sheet C.

PREPARATION & PLEATING

For full instructions, see page 51.

SMOCKING

For full instructions, see pages 51, 53 and 54.

PREPARATION & EMBROIDERY

For full instructions, see pages 53 - 54.

CONSTRUCTION

All seam allowances are 1cm (³/8") unless otherwise specified.

TECHNIQUES USED

BLOCKING SMOCKING, SEE PAGE 114

ATTACHING FLAT FABRIC TO ENTREDEUX, SEE PAGE 95

ATTACHING GATHERED FABRIC TO ENTREDEUX, SEE PAGE 96

ATTACHING FLAT LACE TO FLAT FABRIC, SEE PAGE 94

ATTACHING FLAT LACE TO FLAT LACE, SEE PAGE 94

INSERTING LACE, SEE PAGE 98

FRENCH SEAM, SEE PAGE 114

SETTING IN SLEEVES, SEE PAGE 115

MAKING A CONTINUOUS LAP PLACKET, SEE PAGES 114 - 115

GOWN

front

back

1. Blocking and shaping

Block the smocking following the instructions on page 113. Using a narrow zigzag or short straight stitch, stitch just inside the marked lines around the neckline and armholes on the front. Cut along the marked lines (diag 1).

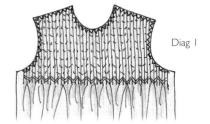

Diag I

2. Preparing the back bodice

Place the wrong side of one organza back bodice onto the right side of one batiste back bodice interlining. Baste the two layers together around all edges *(diag 2)*.

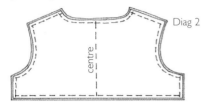

Diag 2

These pieces will be treated as a single layer from now on. Repeat for the remaining back bodice pieces.

3. Shoulder seams

With right sides together and matching raw edges, pin and stitch the front to the back bodice pieces at the shoulders. Repeat for the linings. Press the bodice seams towards the back and the lining seams open *(diag 3)*.

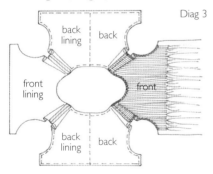

Diag 3

4. Collar

Place two collar pieces wrong sides together. Baste the two layers together around all edges. These will be treated as a single layer from now on.

Measure 3.5cm (1 ³/8") and 7.5cm (3") from one end of the lace edging. Mark at each measurement on the lace heading.

With right sides together, fold the lace so the two measurements meet. Form a mitre at this point *(diag 4)*.

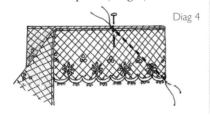

Diag 4

With right sides together, pin and tack the lace to the collar until 1cm (³/8") from the second corner. Form a mitre as before and continue pinning and tacking the lace to the collar. Attach the lace edging to the collar and then work machine pin stitch along the entire seam *(diags 5a and 5b)*. Press.

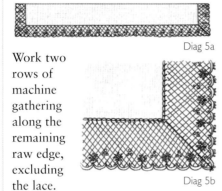

Diag 5a

Work two rows of machine gathering along the remaining raw edge, excluding the lace.

Diag 5b

Make the second collar piece in the same manner.

5. Attaching the collar

Secure the collar pieces together at the centre front *(diag 6)*.

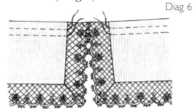

Diag 6

Matching raw edges, centre fronts and centre backs and with the under collar facing the right side of the bodice, pin the collar to the bodice. Pull up the gathering threads to fit the neckline. Baste *(diag 7)*. Ensure the lining is out of the way.

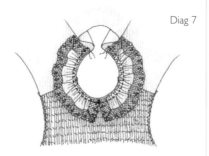

Diag 7

With right sides together and matching raw edges and seams at the neckline, place the lining over the bodice. The collar is sandwiched

between. Pin through all layers. Stitch around the neckline, beginning and ending off securely *(diag 8)*. Trim the seam and clip at approximately 1cm (³/8") intervals.

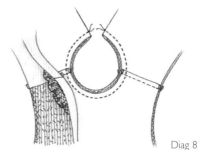

Diag 8

Open out the lining. Keeping the bodice out of the way, understitch around the neckline close to the seam, stitching through the lining and the seam allowance beneath *(diag 9)*.

Fold the lining to the inside and press.

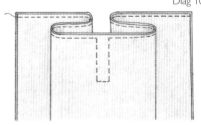

Diag 9

6. Placket

Matching upper and side edges, place the wrong side of the back overskirt to the right side of the back underskirt. tack the two layers together following the diagram *(diag 10)*.

Diag 10

These pieces will be treated as a single layer for making the placket and attaching to the back bodice.

Marking a line measuring 12cm (4 ⁵/8") from the upper edge, make the placket following the instructions on pages 114 - 115.

7. Attaching the back skirt

Work two rows of machine gathering across each half of the back skirt.

Pull up the gathers to fit the back bodice. With right sides together and matching raw edges and centre back foldlines to placket edges, pin each side of the skirt to the corresponding back bodice. Ensure the linings are out of the way and stitch in place (diag 11).

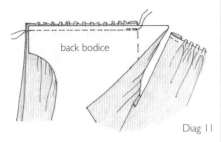

Diag 11

Fold the back bodice linings around the skirt, sandwiching the skirt between the bodice and lining. Pin and stitch along the previous stitchline (diag 12). Trim the seams, turn to the right side and press.

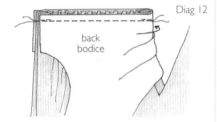

Diag 12

8. First side seam

Matching raw edges and shoulder seams, pin and tack the lining to the bodice around the armholes. Clip the seam on the overskirt just below the back bodice seam (diag 13).

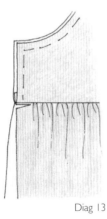

Diag 13

The side seams for the overskirt and underskirt are stitched separately except for a small section under the armholes. With right sides together and matching raw edges, pin the front and back overskirt together along one side. Beginning just below the back bodice seam, stitch (diag 14).

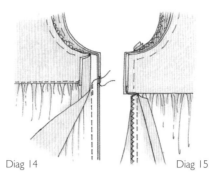

Diag 14   Diag 15

Trim the seam to 3mm (1/8") and neaten. Clip the seam at the end of the stitching (diag 15).

Keeping the overskirt out of the way at the clipped point, pin and stitch the entire underskirt side seam, starting from the armhole (diag 16). (Note: the beginning section of stitching goes through both the overskirt and underskirt). Trim to 5mm (3/16"). Neaten the entire seam. Press the seam towards the back.

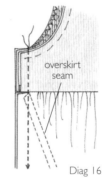

overskirt seam

Diag 16

9. Underskirt

Starting and finishing at the unstitched side seam, attach the wide lace edging to the lower edge of the underskirt.

10. Overskirt

Matching raw edges to placement marks and starting at the unstitched side seam, place the overskirt over the skirt template. Using the fabric marker, mark the positions of the tucks and lace insertion around the entire skirt.

Attach a length of lace insertion to each side of the lace beading (diag 17). Press.

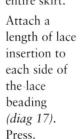

Diag 17

Cut the joined lace into three pieces of equal length.

Pin and tack one piece of joined lace to the right side of the skirt at one marked position. Insert the lace following the instructions on page 98. Attach the two remaining bands of lace in exactly the same manner.

Thread silk ribbon through the lace beading in each band of lace.

11. Finishing the side seams

Stitch the remaining side seams in the same manner as the previous side. When stitching the overskirt, ensure the bands of lace are aligned.

12. Hem and tucks

Fold under 8.5cm (3 3/8") on the lower edge and press. With wrong sides together, fold the overskirt along the mark indicated for the lower tuck. Press. Stitch 2.5cm (1") from the fold. The hem is enclosed in the tuck (diag 18).

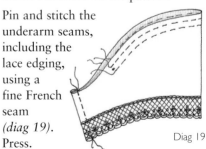

Diag 18

Press and stitch the remaining three tucks. Press the tucks down. Transfer and work the beaded hearts following the instructions on page 53.

13. Sleeves

Matching raw edges, pin and tack the two layers of organza together. These will be treated as one layer from now on. Attach lace edging to the lower edge of each sleeve. Work machine pin stitch along the lace seam.

Stitch two rows of machine gathering across each sleeve head between the marks indicated on the pattern.

Pin and stitch the underarm seams, including the lace edging, using a fine French seam (diag 19). Press.

Diag 19

Set in the sleeves following the instructions on page 115.

14. Finishing

Stitch three buttonholes on the right back bodice at the positions indicated on the pattern. Attach buttons to the left back bodice to correspond.

BOLERO

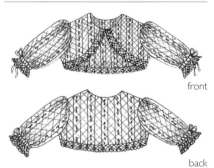

front

back

1. Piecing the lace

Press and spray starch the organza and laces before using them.

Fold the rectangle of organza to find the centre. Mark the fold. Beginning at the centre, place the floral lace insertion on the organza and baste along each side with a machine straight stitch *(diag 1)*. Cut off the excess lace.

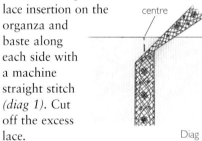

centre

Diag 1

Overlapping the lace headings, pin lace beading along one side of the floral lace insertion. Stitch along the lace headings using a narrow zigzag stitch. Baste the remaining edge of the beading to the organza backing *(diag 2)*.

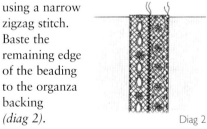

Diag 2

Attach lace beading to the other side of the insertion in the same manner. Working outwards and using the same method as before, attach lace to each side in the following order - diamond insertion, floral insertion, beading, diamond insertion, floral insertion, diamond insertion, floral insertion, diamond insertion and floral insertion *(diag 3)*.

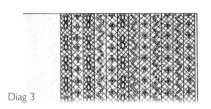

Diag 3

Thread silk ribbon through the lace beading. Cut out all pattern pieces following the cutting layout.

2. Shoulder seams

Cut a length of narrow entredeux the same width as the shoulder. Attach the entredeux to the front shoulder edge following the instructions on page 95. Attach the back shoulder to the remaining edge of the entredeux in the same manner. Press the seams away from the entredeux *(diag 4)*. Repeat for the other shoulder.

Diag 4

3. Side seams

Using a fine French seam, stitch the front to the back at the sides. Press the seams towards the back.

4. Lower edge and neckline

Starting and ending at the centre front, attach lace edging around the entire lower edge of the bolero *(diag 5)*. Press.

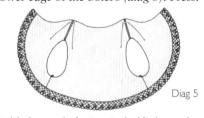

Diag 5

Fold the neck facing in half along the length and press. With right sides together, matching raw edges and with 6mm (¹/₄") extending at each end, pin the doubled facing to the neckline. Stitch, including the ends of the lace edging *(diag 6)*.

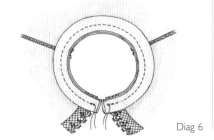

Diag 6

Fold in the ends of the facing and then fold the facing to the inside. Pin and stitch along the folded edge *(diag 7)*.

Diag 7

5. Sleeves

Stitch two rows of machine gathering across the sleeve head between the marks indicated on the pattern. Stitch two more rows across the lower edge of the sleeve *(diag 8)*.

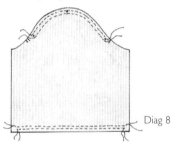

Diag 8

Pull up the gathers on the lower edge to fit the length of entredeux beading. Stitch the lower edge of the sleeve to the beading following the instructions on page 95 *(diag 9)*.

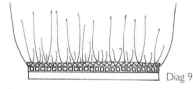

Diag 9

Pull the gimp thread in the heading of the lace edging cut for the sleeve frill and gather to fit the beading. Attach the lace to the beading.

Cut a 50cm (19 ³/₈") length of ribbon and thread through the lace beading, leaving a long loop at the centre *(diag 10)*.

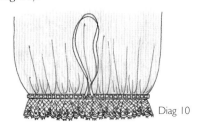

Diag 10

The ends of the ribbon will be secured in the sleeve seam later.

Using a fine French seam, stitch the underarm seam including the sleeve band and frill (diag 11). Press.

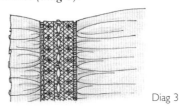

Diag 11

6. Setting in the sleeves

Set in the sleeves following the instructions on page 115.

7. Finishing

Stitch the snap fastener to the top of the lace edging at the centre front. Attach the heart button to the lace edging on the left side.

Cut the ends of the ribbon for the sleeve ties at an angle. Pull up the gathers and tie the ribbons into bows.

BONNET

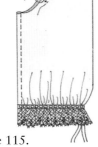

1. Piecing the band

Press and spray starch the laces.

Attach a piece of lace insertion to each side of the lace beading following the instructions on page 94. Attach narrow entredeux to the remaining edge of each piece of insertion following the instructions on page 95. Thread silk ribbon through the lace beading (diag 1).

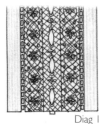

Diag 1

Cut the band to measure 29cm (11 1/2").

2. Joining the frill and bonnet

Work two rows of machine gathering along one long edge of the bonnet piece. Pull up the gathers to fit the band. Attach the bonnet to the entredeux on one side of the band following the instructions on page 96 (diag 2).

Diag 2

With wrong sides together and matching raw edges, baste the two frill pieces together around all edges. These will be treated as one layer from now on.

Gather and attach the frill to the other side of the band in the same manner as the bonnet (diag 3).

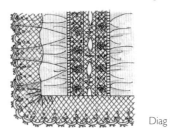

Diag 3

3. Lace edging

Beginning at one back corner, attach the lace edging along one end of the bonnet and band, along the frill and down the other side of the band and bonnet in the same manner as the gown collar. Pull the gimp thread in the lace heading to gather the lace around the corners of the frill (diag 4).

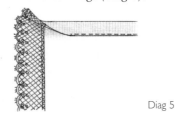

Diag 4

Work machine pin stitch along the lace seam on the frill section only.

4. Casing

Fold under 5mm (3/16") along the back edge of the bonnet, including the lace edging. Press. Fold under a further 1cm (3/8") and press. Stitch close to the folded edge (diag 5).

Diag 5

5. Making the ties

Cut the length of organdie ribbon in half. Fold under 1cm (3/8") at one end of a piece of ribbon. Work tiny running stitches across the ribbon, 5mm (3/16") down from the folded end.

Pull up the stitches to gather the ribbon (diag 6).

Repeat for the remaining tie.

Diag 6

6. Attaching the ties

Centre the gathered end of the ribbon on the right side of the lace beading at one end of the bonnet. Secure with 2 - 3 tiny stitches. Attach a button over the end of the ribbon (diag 7).

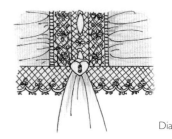

Diag 7

Repeat for the remaining tie. Cut the ends of the ribbon at an angle.

7. Finishing

Thread the silk satin ribbon through the casing at the back of the bonnet. Draw up firmly and tie the ribbon into a bow.

TENDERNESS

For full details and colour photos, see pages 58 - 69.

Sizes 3, 6 and 12 months

REQUIREMENTS

For full details, see pages 60, 61 and 66.

PATTERN & CUTTING OUT

For full details, see liftout pattern sheet C.

PREPARATION & PLEATING

For full instructions, see pages 61 and 66.

SMOCKING

For full instructions, see pages 61 - 63 and 66 - 67.

PREPARATION & EMBROIDERY

For full instructions, see pages 62, 66 and 67.

CONSTRUCTION

All seam allowances are 1cm ($^3/_8$") unless otherwise specified.

GOWN

front

back

1. Blocking and shaping

Block the smocking following the instructions on page 114.

Place the blocking guide over the smocking, aligning the top holding row with the upper stitchline on the guide. Mark the armhole shaping with the fabric marker. Using a narrow zigzag or short straight stitch, stitch just inside the marked lines around the armholes. Cut along the marked lines *(diag 1)*.

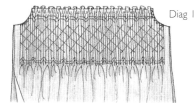

Diag 1

Place the two back overskirt pieces right sides together. Using the back armhole cutting guide, mark and cut out the armhole shaping from one corner through both layers *(diag 2)*. Repeat for the back underskirt.

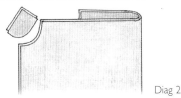

Diag 2

2. Shoulder seams

With right sides together and matching raw edges, pin and stitch the front to the back yoke at the shoulders. Repeat for the linings, forming a circle at the neckline. Press the seams open *(diag 3)*.

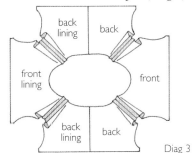

back lining
back
front lining
front
back lining
back

Diag 3

3. Piping the front skirt

Cut a length of piping to fit the lower edge of the front yoke. Pin the piping to the right side of the front skirt, aligning the stitchline on the piping with the top holding row. Tack and stitch in place along the piping stitchline *(diag 4)*.

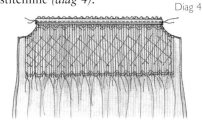

Diag 4

4. Attaching the front skirt

With right sides together and matching centres, pin the piped skirt to the lower edge of the front yoke. Stitch between the corded edge of the piping and the previous stitchline *(diag 5)*. Trim the seam and press towards the yoke.

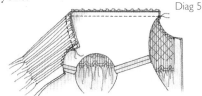

Diag 5

5. Button bands

Fold under 2.5cm (1") on the back overskirt opening edge and press. Fold under a further 2.5cm (1") and press. Baste across the top edge of the button band just inside the seam allowance. Repeat on the remaining back overskirt piece and the two back underskirt pieces *(diag 6)*.

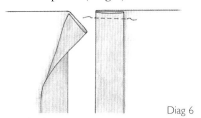

Diag 6

6. Back skirt

Matching raw edges and back opening edges, place the wrong side of one overskirt onto the right side of the corresponding underskirt and pin. The two layers are treated as one while attaching them to the back yoke.

7. Attaching the back skirt

Stitch two rows of machine gathering across the top of the back skirt. Pull up the gathers to fit the lower edge of the back yoke. Do not gather the button band. Repeat for the remaining half of the back skirt.

With right sides together and matching raw edges, pin each side of the back skirt to the corresponding back yoke. Ensure the linings are out of the way and stitch in place (diag 7).

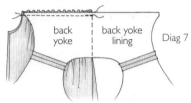

back yoke   back yoke lining   Diag 7

Fold the linings around the skirt, sandwiching the skirt between. Pin and stitch along the previous stitchline (diag 8). Trim the seams, turn to the right side and press.

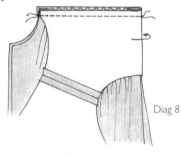

Diag 8

8. Securing the lining

Press under the seam allowance on the lower edge of the front lining. With wrong sides together and matching raw edges and shoulder seams, tack the lining to the yoke around the neckline and armholes (see diag 9).

Align the folded edge of the front yoke lining with the skirt stitchline and hand stitch in place (diag 9).

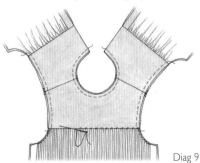

Diag 9

9. Piping and binding the neckline

Cut a piece of piping the same length as the neck binding. Matching centres and with raw edges even, pin the piping to the right side of the neckline, allowing 1cm (3/8") of piping to extend past the back opening edges. Trim away any excess. Pin and stitch along the piping stitchline (diag 10).

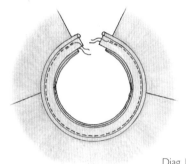

Diag 10

With wrong sides together, fold the neck binding in half along the length and press. Matching raw edges, pin the doubled binding to the neckline over the piping, stretching the binding slightly. Leave 1cm (3/8") extending beyond the back opening edges. Trim away any excess. With the lining uppermost, stitch between the corded edge of the piping and the previous stitchline (diag 11).

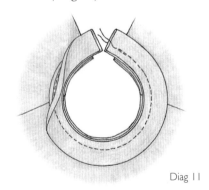

Diag 11

Stitch again 5mm (3/16") away from the seam. Trim very close to the second row of stitching.

Fold in the extended ends of the piping and binding, tucking the piping tails up into the seam allowance (see diag 12). Firmly fold the binding over the seam allowance to the wrong side. Pin and hand stitch the binding in place (diag 12).

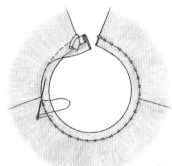

Diag 12

10. Side seams

The side seams for the overskirt and underskirt are stitched separately. With wrong sides together and matching raw edges, pin the front and back overskirts together at the sides. Stitch using a fine French seam (diag 13).

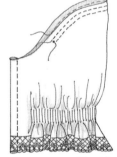

Diag 13

Press the seams towards the back. Repeat for the underskirt side seams. Tack the overskirt and underskirt together at the underarms.

11. Sleeves

Stitch two rows of machine gathering across each sleeve head between the marks indicated on the pattern.

Pin and stitch the underarm seams, including the lace, using a fine French seam (diag 14). Press.

Diag 14

Set in the sleeves following the instructions on page 115.

12. Lower overskirt

Open out the button bands on the lower edge of the overskirt. Attach the lace edging to the lower edge following the instructions on page 94. Press the lace downwards and the seam towards the skirt.

Press and spray starch the lower section of the skirt. Place the skirt over the hem template. Transfer the placement marks for the pintucks and embroidery following the instructions on page 62.

Stitch the twin needle pintucks and work the embroidery.

13. Lower underskirt

Attach lace edging to the lower edge in the same manner as the overskirt.

Transfer and work the embroidery following the instructions on pages 62 and 67.

14. Finishing

Remove all traces of the fabric marker. Refold the button bands on the overskirt and press. Hand stitch the button bands in place (diag 15).

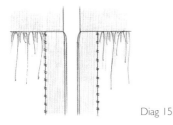

Diag 15

Repeat for the button bands on the underskirt.

Matching folded edges, tack the overskirt to the underskirt at the back opening edges for approximately 25cm (10"). These will be treated as one layer for working the buttonholes and attaching the buttons.

Stitch two buttonholes on the right back yoke at the positions indicated on the pattern. Stitch three more buttonholes on the upper section of the right back button band spacing them approximately 8cm (3 1/8") apart. Attach buttons to the left back yoke and skirt to correspond.

BONNET

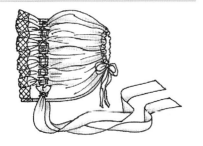

1. Making the ties

With right sides together, fold one tie in half along the length. Stitch down the long side and diagonally across one end. Trim the seam and clip the corners (diag 1).

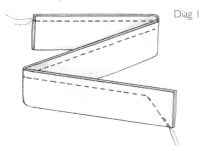

Diag 1

Turn to the right side and press. Fold in the raw edge at the end of the tie and press. Hand stitch the opening closed (diag 2).

Make the remaining tie in the same manner.

Diag 2

2. Attaching the ties

Measure down 1.5cm (5/8") from the squared end of the tie and mark. Work a row of tiny running stitches across the tie at this measurement

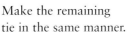

1.5cm

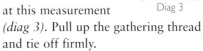

Diag 3

(diag 3). Pull up the gathering thread and tie off firmly.

Place the tie on the right side of the bonnet. Position it so the gathering is just in from the finished edge of the bonnet and the tie is aligned with the smocking (diag 4).

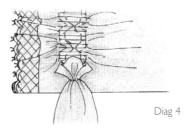

Diag 4

Secure with 2 - 3 small stitches. Repeat for the remaining tie.

Work the bullion roses following the instructions on pages 66 - 67.

3. Making the ribbon for the crown

Fold the bias cut fabric in half along the length. Stitch 6mm (1/4") from the folded edge. Trim the seam. Turn to the right side and press. Fold in both ends and hand stitch the openings closed.

4. Finishing

Thread the ribbon through the casing at the back of the bonnet. Draw up firmly and tie into a bow.

HUSH

For full details and colour photos, see pages 70 - 77.

Sizes 3, 6 and 12 months

REQUIREMENTS

For full details, see pages 72, 73 & 75.

PATTERN & CUTTING OUT

For full instructions, see liftout pattern sheet A.

PREPARATION & PLEATING

For full instructions, see pages 73 & 75.

SMOCKING

For full instructions, see pages 74 & 75.

CONSTRUCTION

All seam allowances are 1cm (3/8") unless otherwise specified.

TECHNIQUES USED

BLOCKING THE SMOCKING,
SEE PAGE 114

MAKING A PIPED COLLAR,
SEE PAGE 114

SETTING IN SLEEVES,
SEE PAGE 115

JACKET

front

back

1. Blocking and shaping

Block the smocking to fit the front blocking guide following the instructions on page 114.

Place the front blocking guide over the smocking on one panel with the stitchline on the upper edge positioned midway between rows 1 and 2. Mark the armhole shaping with the fabric marker. Flipping the blocking guide, repeat on the remaining panel.

Using a narrow zigzag or short straight stitch, stitch just inside the marked lines around the armholes. Cut along the marked lines (diag 1).

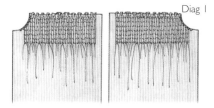

Diag 1

Place the two front lining pieces right sides together. Using the front blocking guide, mark and cut the armhole shaping from one corner through both layers.

With right sides together, fold the jacket back in half down the length. Using the back armhole cutting guide, mark and cut the shaping in the upper corner opposite the fold (diag 2). Repeat for the back lining.

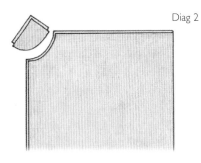

Diag 2

2. Preparing the button bands

On both the front yoke and front yoke lining, staystitch around the inner corner on the stitchline (diag 3).

Fuse interfacing to the wrong side of the button band on both the left and right front pieces. Clip into the corner almost up to the stitching on both the button band and lining pieces.

Diag 3

3. Shoulder seams

With right sides together and matching raw edges, pin and stitch the front to the back yoke pieces at the shoulders (diag 4).

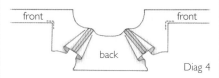

front   front

back

Diag 4

Repeat for the linings. Press the seams open.

4. Collar

Make the piped collar following the general instructions on page 114.

Matching raw edges, centre fronts and centre backs and with the under collar facing the right side of the yoke, pin and tack the collar to the yoke. Stitch (diag 5).

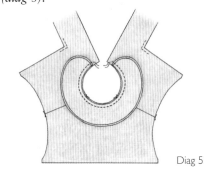

Diag 5

With right sides together and matching raw edges and seams at the neckline, place the lining over the yoke. The collar is sandwiched between. Pin through all layers. Stitch around the neckline, beginning and ending off securely (diag 6).

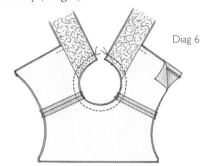

Diag 6

Trim the seam and clip at approximately 1cm ($^3/_8$") intervals.

5. Piping the front

Cut two lengths of piping to fit the lower edge of the left front yoke and button band. Matching stitchlines, pin the piping to the right side of the front yoke and button band, clipping the piping heading at the reinforced corner (diag 7).

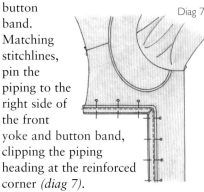

Diag 7

On the button band, curve the end of the piping into the seam allowance 1cm ($^3/_8$") from the lower edge (diag 8).

Stitch along the piping stitchline. Repeat on the remaining front.

Diag 8

Cut two lengths of piping to fit the outer edge of the button band. Matching stitchlines, pin the piping to the right side of the band. Curve the ends of the piping into the seam allowance 1cm ($^3/_8$") from the lower edge and the stitchline at the upper edge. Stitch along the piping stitchline (diag 9).

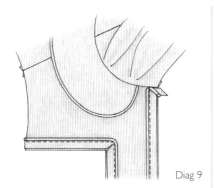

Diag 9

6. Attaching the smocked fronts

Neaten the lower edge of each smocked front. Fold under 3.5cm (1 $^3/_8$") on the lower edges and press *(see diag 10)*.

With right sides together and matching raw edges, pin the front yoke and button band to the corresponding smocked front. The folded lower edge of the front is 1cm ($^3/_8$") from the lower raw edge of the band. Stitch between the corded edge of the piping and the previous stitchline. Trim and neaten the seam. Press towards the yoke and button band *(diag 10)*. Attach the remaining smocked front in the same manner.

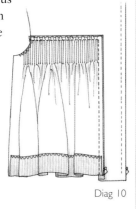

Diag 10

Understitch around the neckline through the lining and the seam allowance beneath *(diag 11)*.

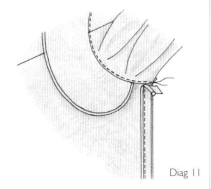

Diag 11

Fold the lining to the inside. Press the neckline gently.

7. Attaching the back

Cut a length of piping to fit the lower edge of the back yoke.

Matching raw edges, pin the piping to the right side of the back yoke. Stitch along the piping stitchline *(diag 12)*.

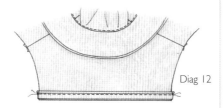

Diag 12

Stitch two rows of machine gathering along the upper edge of the jacket back. Pull up the gathering threads to fit the back yoke.

With right sides together and matching raw edges, pin the yoke to the jacket back. The piping is sandwiched between. Stitch, ensuring the lining is out of the way *(diag 13)*.

Diag 13

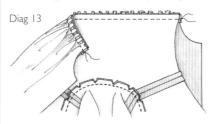

Trim the seam and press towards the yoke.

8. Side seams

With right sides together and matching raw edges, pin the front and back together at the sides. Stitch *(diag 14)*.

Diag 14

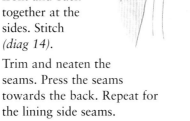

Trim and neaten the seams. Press the seams towards the back. Repeat for the lining side seams.

Neaten the lower edge of the jacket back.

9. Lining

Fold under 1cm ($^3/_8$") on the lower edge and press. Fold under a further 1cm ($^3/_8$") and press. Machine stitch the hem.

Stitch two rows of machine gathering along the upper edge of each lining piece. Pull up the gathers to fit the yoke lining pieces.

With right sides together and matching raw edges, pin and stitch one front lining to the corresponding front yoke and button band lining *(diag 15)*.

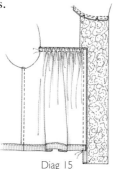

Diag 15

Attach the remaining front lining in the same manner. With right sides together, pin and stitch the back yoke lining to the back lining. Trim the seam and press towards the yoke.

With right sides together and matching raw edges, pin the button band lining to the outer edge of the button band. Stitch down the front opening edge and across the lower end *(diag 16)*.

Trim the seam, clip the corners, turn to the right side and press. Repeat for the remaining side. Tack the lining and jacket together around the armholes.

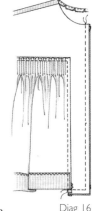

Diag 16

10. Jacket hem

Fold under a 3.5cm (1 $^3/_8$") hem and press. Hand stitch the hem in place.

11. Sleeves

With right sides together and matching raw edges, pin and stitch a sleeve cuff to the lower edge of one sleeve lining *(diag 17)*. Press the seam open.

Diag 17

Cut two lengths of piping to fit the lower edge of the sleeve. Pin piping to the right side of the sleeve, curving the ends into the seam allowance 1cm ($^3/_8$") in from each side *(diag 18)*.

Stitch along the piping stitchline.

With right sides together and matching raw edges, pin and stitch the cuff to the sleeve. The piping is sandwiched between. Trim the seam and press.

Diag 18

With right sides together, pin and stitch the underarm seam in both the sleeve and lining (diag 19).

Press the seam open. Push the lining into the sleeve. Repeat for the remaining sleeve. Stitching through both the sleeve and lining, stitch two rows of machine gathering across each sleeve head between the marks indicated on the pattern.

Diag 19

12. Setting in the sleeves

Set in the sleeves following the instructions on page 115.

13. Finishing

Turn up 2.5cm (1") at the lower edge of each sleeve to form the cuffs. Press. Secure the tops of the cuffs to the sleeves at the underarm seam with several hand stitches.

Hand stitch the lower section of the button band lining to the hem (diag 20). Press. Repeat on the opposite side.

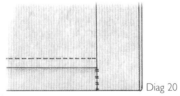

Diag 20

Cover the buttons with the satin fabric, following the manufacturer's instructions.

Stitch 4 - 5 buttonholes on the right button band at the positions indicated on the pattern. Attach buttons to the left button band to correspond. Attach the snap fastener to the button band at the position indicated on the pattern.

PANTS

front   back

1. Joining the front to the back

With right sides together and matching raw edges, pin and stitch the centre front seam (diag 1). Stitch the centre front seam again to reinforce. Clip the curve and press the seam open. Repeat for the back pieces.

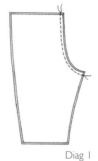

Diag 1

With right sides together and matching raw edges, pin and stitch the front to the back at the sides (diag 2). Press the seams open.

Diag 2

2. Lining

Assemble the lining in the same manner as the pants, leaving an opening in the centre back seam at the position marked on the pattern.

3. Cuffs

With right sides together and matching raw edges, pin and stitch a cuff to the lower edge of each leg of the lining (diag 3).

Diag 3

Press the seam towards the lining.

Cut two lengths of piping to fit the lower leg edge. Matching raw edges, pin one piece of piping to the right side of one lower leg. Curve the ends of the piping into the seam allowance. Stitch along the piping stitchline (diag 4).

Diag 4

Attach piping to the remaining lower leg in the same manner. Place the lining and pants right sides together, sandwiching the piping between the two layers. Pin and stitch across the lower legs, stitching between the corded edge of the piping and the previous stitchline (diag 5). Trim the seam. Turn to the right side and press.

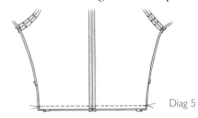

Diag 5

4. Inside leg seams

Stitch the inside leg seam in both the pants and the lining (diag 6). Bring the top of the pants inside leg seam to meet the top of the lining inside leg seam. Turn the pants right side out covering the lining (diag 7).

lining

pants

Diag 6

Ensure the piping sits along the fold at the lower edge of the legs.

5. Waistband

Diag 7

Fold under 1cm ($^3/_8$") at the waist and press. Matching seams and folded edges pin the the pants to the lining.

Stitch around the upper edge close to the fold. Stitch again 2.5cm (1") from the folded edge *(diag 8)*.

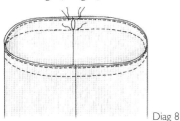

Diag 8

As a guide, cut the elastic to -
Size 3 months: 39cm (15 3/8")
Size 6 months: 40cm (15 3/4")
Size 12 months: 41cm (16 1/8").

Alternatively, measure the waist of the baby.

Thread the elastic through the casing. Overlap the ends and securely stitch them together. Hand stitch the opening closed.

6. Finishing

Turn up each leg 3cm (1 1/8") to form the cuffs. Press. Secure the tops of the cuffs to the pants at the inside and outside leg seams with several hand stitches.

BERET

1. Blocking

Remove the pleating threads except for the holding row. Block the smocked band to measure 49cm (19 1/4"), following the instructions on page 114.

2. Making the crown

Cut six pieces of piping, each 14.5cm (5 5/8") long. Matching raw edges and one end of the piping with the outer edge of the crown section, pin a length of piping to one straight edge of the crown section. Curve the other end of the piping so it tapers away from the stitch-line 2cm (3/4") from the tip of the crown. Stitch along the piping stitchline *(diag 1)*.

Diag 1

With right sides together and matching raw edges, pin a second crown section to the piped edge of the first

section. The piping is sandwiched between. Stitch between the corded edge of the piping and the previous stitch-line *(diag 2)*. Trim the seam and press to one side.

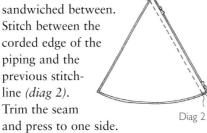

Diag 2

Continue piping and joining the crown sections until you form a complete circle *(diag 3)*. Following the manufacturer's instructions, cover the button with cream satin fabric. Secure the button to the centre of the crown.

Diag 3

3. Joining the band and brim

With right sides together, join the ends of the smocked band to form a circle. Trim the seam and neaten both sides separately. Press the seam open. Hand stitch the edges to the band *(diag 4)*.

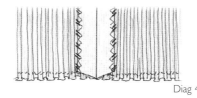

Diag 4

With right sides together and aligning the stitchline on the brim just above the smocking, pin the raw edge of the smocked band to the inner edge of the brim. Use the pleating thread to ease it to fit. Stitch *(diag 5)*. Trim the seam and press towards the brim.

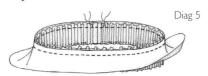

Diag 5

4. Attaching the crown to the brim

Beginning at the centre back, pin piping to the right side of the crown around the outer edge, clipping the heading as required. Overlap the ends of the piping and curve them into the seam allowance. Stitch *(diag 6)*.

With right sides together and aligning the seam in the band with the join in the piping, pin the brim to the crown. The piping is sandwiched between. Stitch *(diag 7)*. Trim the seam and clip the curves. Press.

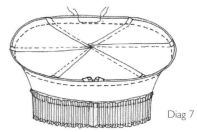

Diag 6

Diag 7

5. Lining

With right sides together and matching raw edges, pin the crown to the outer edge of the brim lining. Stitch. Trim the seam and clip the curves. Press.

6. Attaching the lining

With the right side of the lining against the wrong side of the smocked band and matching seams, position the lining over the beret. The smocked band is sandwiched between. Pin and stitch around the inner edge of the brim leaving a 7cm (2 3/4") opening in the stitching *(diag 8)*.

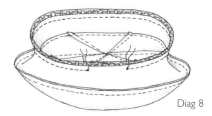

Diag 8

Trim the seam. Turn to the right side through the opening. Hand stitch the opening closed *(diag 9)*.

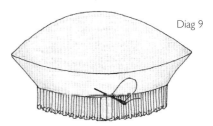

Diag 9

NOW BE EVEN MORE INSPIRED

At *Country Bumpkin* our aim is to inspire people to actively participate in the wonderful world of needlework.
These beautiful books and magazines are as close as the phone, internet and your letterbox.

THE A-Z SERIES

These creative books, which have sold more than 2,000,000 copies, will give you fresh ideas and renewed confidence. Featuring beautifully presented step-by-step instructions, stunning photography and glorious designs for you to stitch, they are the ultimate reference books for needleworkers.

A-Z of Embroidered Flowers

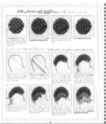
A-Z of Embroidery Stitches

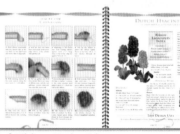
A-Z of Ribbon Embroidery

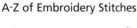
A-Z of Bullions

A-Z of Sewing for Smockers

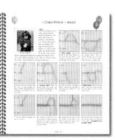
A-Z of Smocking

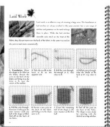
A-Z of Crewel Embroidery

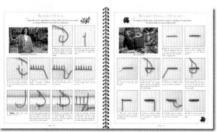
A-Z of Wool Embroidery

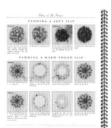
A-Z of Stumpwork

QUARTERLY MAGAZINES

Each magazine features stunning projects, magnificent photography, clear step-by-step instructions and full size patterns.

Inspirations
The World's Most Beautiful Embroidery

Australian Smocking & Embroidery
More than just a magazine

NEEDLEWORK BOOKS

Filled with beautiful projects, easy instructions, superb photography and full size patterns.

Inspirations Baby

Inspirations Bridal

Inspirations Gifts

The World's Most Beautiful
Embroidered Blankets

Embroidered Bags and Purses

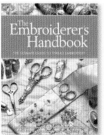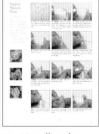

The Embroiderer's Handbook

The Embroidered Village Bag

How to order

It's really quite simple to order any or all of these quality books and magazines.

Phone

08 8372 7600 within Australia or **61 8 8372 7600** from overseas and speak to our helpful team who will process your order promptly.

Fax

Fax your order with payment and address details to **08 8372 7601** within Australia or **61 8 8372 7601** from overseas.

Internet

Email
mailorder@countrybumpkin.com.au
or log on to
www.countrybumpkin.com.au
and follow the simple steps to order.

Visit

Country Bumpkin Shop
315 Unley Rd, Malvern
South Australia 5061
Phone (08) 8372 7676

A Bush Christening

ANDREW   BARTON   'BANJO'   PATERSON

On the outer Barcoo where the churches are few,
And men of religion are scanty,
On a road never cross'd 'crept by folk that are lost,
One Michael Magee had a shanty.

Now this Mike was the dad of a ten year old lad,
Plump, healthy, and stoutly conditioned;
He was strong as the best, but poor Mike had no rest
For the youngster had never been christened.

And his wife used to cry, "If the darlin' should die
Saint Peter would not recognise him."
But by luck he survived till a preacher arrived,
Who agreed straightaway to baptise him.

Now the artful young rouge, while they held their collogue,
With his ear to the keyhole was listenin',
And he muttered in fright, while his features turned white,
"What the divil and all is this christenin'?"

He was none of your dolts, he had seen them brand colts,
And it seemed to his small understanding,
If the man in the frock made him one of the flock,
It must mean something very like branding.

So away with a rush he set off for the bush,
While the tears in his eyelids they glistened -
"'Tis outrageous," says he, "to brand youngsters like me,
I'll be dashed if I'll stop to be christened!"

Like a young native dog he ran into a log,
And his father with language uncivil,
Never heeding the "praste" cried aloud in his haste,
"Come out and be christened, you divil!"

But he lay there as snug as a bug in a rug,
And his parents in vain might reprove him,
Till his reverence spoke (he was fond of a joke)
"I've a notion," says he, "that'll move him."

Poke a stitch up the log, give a spalpeen a prog;
Poke him aisy – don't hurt him or maim him,
'Tis not long that he'll stand, I've water at hand,
As he rushes out this end I'll name him.

"Here he comes, and for shame! ye've forgotten the name -
Is it Patsy or Michael or Dinnis?"
Here the youngster ran out, and the priest gave a shout -
"Take your chance, anyhow, wid 'Maginnis'!"

As the howling young cub ran away to the scrub
Where he knew that pursuit would be risky,
The priest, as he fled, flung a flask at his head
That was labelled "Maginnis's Whisky"!

And Maginnis Magee has been made a J.P.,
And the one thing he hates more than sin is
To be asked by the folk, who have heard of the joke,
How he came to be christened Maginnis!